GUERRILLA
SOCIAL MEDIA
MARKETING

100+ Weapons to
Grow Your Online Influence,
Attract Customers,
and Drive Profits

@••••

#••••

JAY CONRAD LEVINSON
SHANE GIBSON

Foreword by Guy Kawasaki

Ep
Entrepreneur
Press

Jere L. Calmes, Publisher
Cover Design: Andrew Welyczko
Production and Composition: Eliot House Productions

This publication is designed to provide accurate and authoritative information in
regard to the subject matter covered. It is sold with the understanding that the
publisher is not engaged in rendering legal, accounting or other professional services. If legal advice or other expert assistance is required, the services of a compe-
tent professional person should be sought.

Library of Congress Cataloging-in-Publication Data
 Levinson, Jay Conrad.
  Guerrilla social media marketing: 100+ weapons to grow your online
 influence, attract customers/by Jay Conrad Levinson and Shane Gibson.
   p. cm.
  ISBN-13: 978-1-59918-383-1 (alk. paper)
  ISBN-10: 1-59918-383-8
    1. Internet marketing. 2. Customer relations. 3. Social media—Marketing.
 I. Gibson, Shane. II. Title.
 HF5415.1265.L4812 2010
 658.8'72—dc22   2010017650

Printed in USA

21 20 19 18 17   12 11 10 9 8

CONTENTS

Contents

ACKNOWLEDGMENTS

 No guerrilla achieves any level of greatness without community and supporters. Writing this book was no different. The support, insight, and contribution came from many people and organizations. We would like to acknowledge the following people for their tremendous support.

Although we connected virtually by web and telephone, it was Cristina Gonzales of Seminarium, Chile, who put us together as guest speakers in April 2009 at a conference in Santiago, Chile. It was there with the encouragement of Jay's wife Jeannie Levinson that the seed for *Guerrilla Social Media Marketing* was planted.

Social media mavens and enthusiasts in our lives were critical: Christy Huffman and Sage Schofield constantly encouraged and shared insights with Jay. Stephen Jagger of Ubertor.com truly introduced Shane to the power of online social networks. James Laitenin, managing director of the International Internet Marketing Association, provided his technical editing and research support.

Friends and family, as always, were vital to our efforts. Jay's wife Jeannie gave her unwavering support and belief. Shane's son Kristian Xavier Gibson was a big supporter of his Dad and his guerrilla projects. Lorraine "Raincoaster" Murphy, Shane's personal editorial assistant, and Lynn Kitchen both burned the midnight oil to make this book possible. Shane's personal support network of business associates including but not limited to Marc Smith, Robert Palkowski, George Moen, Dr. Raul Pacheco-Vega, Ross Bailey, Christine Van, and David Huska are all true guerrillas and leaders in their own unique way.

Finally, we recognize the support of our guerrilla community. We would need an entire book just to list all of the innovators and leaders who have inspired us with their tweets, blog entries, personal meetings, and innovative marketing ideas. For leading the way, we thank you.

—Jay Conrad Levinson and Shane Gibson

HOW TO BECOME A SOCIAL MEDIA GUERRILLA

BY GUY KAWASAKI

I first met Jay Conrad Levinson, the father of guerrilla marketing, when I interviewed him in the early '90s. I met Shane Gibson at an Olympic Hockey Tweetup in Vancouver, Canada. When Shane told me that he and Jay were working on this latest volume of the *Guerrilla Marketing* series about social media, he caught my interest because the two are a match made in heaven.

Alltop, an "online magazine rack" that I co-founded, owes its success to social media guerilla marketing. We used Twitter and Facebook to create Alltop evangelists, galvanize our supporters and critics, and generate page views and brand awareness. We also tapped community and built multiple nano-casts of content for the nano-markets that Jay and Shane talk about in this book.

The combination of the social media and guerilla marketing enables entrepreneurs to level the playing field in their industry. Capitalizing on social media outlets is not just about using them as tools but taking matters beyond this and making them guerilla-marketing weapons.

Jay and Shane have crafted a comprehensive guide for the marketer, entrepreneur, or executive that is serious about profiting from social media. The challenges that people face in social media are:

- ➤ What tools to use and how to use them profitably.
- ➤ Finding and engaging profitable target markets.
- ➤ How to build community and then raving fans.
- ➤ What and how to measure ROI.

This book answers all these issues. It's not an easy path; it will take discipline, tenacity, and creativity. For those who are willing to pay this price, Jay and Shane have provided the ultimate roadmap needed to achieve your goal.

—Guy Kawasaki

Guy Kawasaki is a founding partner and entrepreneur-in-residence at Garage Technology Ventures. He is also the co-founder of Alltop.com, an "online magazine rack" of popular topics on the web. Previously, he was an Apple Fellow at Apple Computer, Inc. Guy is the author of nine books including *Reality Check, The Art of the Start, Rules for Revolutionaries, How to Drive Your Competition Crazy, Selling the Dream,* and *The Macintosh Way.* He has a BA from Stanford University and an MBA from UCLA as well as an honorary doctorate from Babson College.

PREFACE

The term "guerrilla marketing" was coined in 1984. The original book and seminar were developed to help creative, entrepreneurial individuals compete with big companies and market leaders. These entrepreneurial marketers were lacking what at the time was considered mandatory: deep pockets.

Large companies and established players dominated the marketplace. They could afford large media buys, expensive brochures, beautiful trade show booths, and armies of salespeople.

Entrepreneurs with very few assets and great ideas were looking for creative ways to enter the marketplace without a big budget or large staff. *Guerrilla Marketing* fulfilled that need.

Guerrilla marketing was and is about using unconventional means to achieve conventional goals. It's about using creativity, innovation, community, and relationships instead of big budgets to achieve marketing objectives.

A few things have changed since 1984. The *Guerrilla Marketing* series of books has now sold over 20 million copies, and guerrilla marketing is a methodology which is now used by companies big and small. The world of marketing has also changed, and big-budget marketers no longer hold the power or have the influence they used to.

We are at the nexus of a time of great change in the world of marketing. Master marketers and advertising industry gurus are becoming less relevant by the second. Soon there will be no more marketing gurus. Every individual is now armed with highly effective online communications tools that enable them to garner the same level of influence that many large corporations have.

The era of social media has changed the marketing landscape even more. No longer are big ad budgets or well-crafted PR campaigns sufficient. With a large measure of creativity and a willingness to authentically engage your customers online, you can now grab mind share and wallet share away from the competition by using largely free and easy-to-use social media marketing weapons.

Social media is something new and foreign. It's misunderstood by many business owners and executives. This book's sole purpose is to cut through the hype and give you easy-to-implement strategies, insights, and tools to help you propel your brand and business into a leading market position.

Social media marketing as a discipline has seen the rise of many gurus, experts, and evangelists. Many are passionate but few are profitable. What is wrong with most social media marketing is that marketers in the space are typically comprised of two groups. The first group is technologically literate people who use these tools for social interaction and to connect with other people. The challenge for this group is they may have a lot of website traffic, many contacts on Twitter, Facebook, or other groups, but they don't understand marketing and struggle to find a return on investment for all of their socializing.

The second group is comprised of traditional marketing agencies, marketing experts, and even people who have succeeded as internet marketers prior to the advent of social media. The big agency type marketers and the corporate types often move into the space with big budgets broadcasting specials and sales, and trying to control their message. The challenge is that very few understand that the conversations about their brand define their brand. It's not big-budget advertising and beautiful video that help people in the social media. What most people are missing is the understanding of the importance of conversation and guerrilla nano-casting strategies.

Successful internet marketers have been able to make money understanding and manipulating search engine algorithms and systems that direct traffic run by computers. Many struggle to get a full return on investment on social media because there's no algorithm; there are only networks of real people voting and communicating about you and your messages. You have to engage genuinely at a very human level to win.

Guerrilla social media marketers understand that social media is social. They know how to hyper target and listen to nano-tribes and communities. Guerrillas know that listening and competitive intelligence are their first lines of attack and defense. They use the size of their competitors against them by being fluid, creative, and genuine. They also succeed through building genuine relationships one at a time, something that has nothing to do with robots or algorithms. If you're passionate, creative, and measure results by profit and not clicks, visits, or gross revenues, this book is your road map to becoming a guerrilla social media marketer.

Social media is a tool to help you connect and communicate directly with your customers and prospects in real time. It can give you access and visibility that most companies could not afford to buy. It also allows you to leverage networks of thousands of people or connect intimately with key customers in a small, focused geographic region. It can be whatever you need it to be, providing you understand the principles of guerrilla social media marketing. *Guerrilla Social Media Marketing* is a step-by-step social media launch guide for entrepreneurs and businesspeople. It applies the time-proven strategies and principles of guerrilla marketing to the new media landscape.

Many of you will already be using social media but have not been able to generate the results you aspired to when you began. You may already have competitors that are well ahead of you in the effective use of these tools. An equal number of you will be those who are not yet using social media but want an effective and easy-to-understand process for getting started. This guide will help you catch up and dominate the market by applying the use of social media in an innovative, unique, guerrilla fashion, complete with action plans, checklists, and implementation steps.

CHAPTER 1

THE GUERRILLA
SOCIAL MEDIA
MARKETER'S PATH

Guerrilla marketing is about achieving conventional goals using unconventional means. Instead of spending large sums of money on traditional mainstream broadcast media, guerrillas use cost-efficient, creative, and innovative strategies to rise above their competition. Today, more than any other time in history, we have an almost limitless arsenal of free or nearly free marketing tools at our fingertips. These tools are the new media marketing tools of this millennium, and they're called "social media."

Social media is a set of tools and websites that are free or nearly free and allow marketers and the community to create content and meaningful conversations online. They include blogs, photo-sharing sites, video-sharing sites, social networks, audio podcasts, and internet radio shows as well as a wide selection of mobile social sharing and communications tools. The conversations and content created by communities and those marketers that engage them are having a huge impact on brands, communities, and the consumer.

Much hyped, promoted, misunderstood, and maligned, social media marketing is a complex multidimensional set of tools, networks, and media. There are many paths to take in the realm of social media marketing. PR people will argue that social media marketing is best left to them. The VP of marketing, the customer service department, and especially your legal department will also argue that they are, in fact, the ones that should be in charge of social media marketing for any company.

What most executives, marketing professionals, and ad agencies fail to realize is that marketing now belongs to everyone, and everyone must be equipped and engaged in the social media space. Your customer with two Tweets, a video blog, and a Facebook status update can do more good or harm to your brand than one of your well-planned marketing campaigns.

DAVE CARROLL

GUERRILLA SOCIAL MEDIA MARKETING PIONEER

UNITED BREAKS GUITARS

Nova Scotian Dave Carroll and his band Sons of Maxwell produced a series of videos with the theme "United Breaks Guitars." They produced the first video after nine frustrating months of trying to get

United Airlines to pay for damage done by their baggage handlers to Dave's Taylor guitar. It wasn't a question of fault; several witnesses in the plane saw handlers recklessly throwing the guitars about the baggage loading area.

Of course, the words "policy," "protocol," and many other things that mean "we're not paying you for the damage that was done" were uttered. After exhausting the United customer service bureaucracy labyrinth, Dave decided not to quit. Instead he put his guerrilla hat on and got creative and innovative. He recruited the help of some friends in video production and produced a very catchy and humorous music video telling of his plight. Within the first 24 hours of the video being on YouTube, it had several hundred thousand views. As of this writing, it had gotten almost ten million views and was growing daily.

Some experts even speculated that the drop in United's share value the next day was partially due to so many views of the negative video. Dave was soon on every major television network and in every major newspaper. This one customer, with a video camera, a catchy tune, and a free YouTube account had rebranded the company that "flies the friendly skies" to one that "breaks guitars."

This is the power of social media. Your customers, your competitors, and everyone in between can be a Dave Carroll and so can you.

Eventually United conceded, but the guitar was already fixed and the damage to its good name was already done. The reality is that, according to United, it has a 99.5 percent success rate for handling bags. The problem is, people will believe their friendly musician friend Dave, not a stat pushed out by a big company.

There are many trails to be blazed in social media. Some will build communities that raise money for charity, others like Barack Obama's online campaign will turn the tide of opinion. The guerrilla social media marketing path is one that is blazed with a keen focus on community, innovation, engagement, and—most importantly—profit. The guerrilla path has a beginning but unless you sell your business or retire, it has no ending. It is a way of doing business and engaging the marketplace that drives real long-term business results. This is not a book on clever marketing campaigns or short-term Facebook contests. The guerrilla path in social media marketing is not easy; in fact it encompasses a set of principles, traits, and attitudes that take work to understand, master, and implement. Still, if you master and implement what you learn in this book, it will be almost impossible for you to fail.

Anyone can become a successful guerrilla social media marketer, but they must want to be one. They must also commit to the personal transformation and work that is necessary to get there. Beyond attitudes, marketing weapons, and plans, we must have the right personality traits to become successful.

THE TEN PERSONALITY TRAITS OF A GUERRILLA SOCIAL MEDIA MARKETER

In the following pages you will learn the personality traits of a guerrilla social media marketer. It will be up to you whether or not these traits describe who you are or who you want to become; you will have to make a decision as to whether or not this doctrine of marketing is for you. It's not an easy path, but the rewards are huge.

1. Immune to Hype

There is a lot of hype around social media. The guerrilla searches for truth, verifies information, and executes with dependable tools and strategies. With so many people blasting Twitter updates, sharing Facebook messages, and posting blog entries, it's easy to get caught up in the excitement of a new product, tool, or market and dive in headfirst. Here's why guerrillas don't fall into this trap:

- Any new social media marketing tool or community takes time, energy, and resources to test and evaluate effectively.
- Great technology alone doesn't mean a marketing tool is worth investing in. The tool must be backed by a great company and have the potential for longevity.
- While you chase every trend and new tool, you neglect communities and marketing tools that need focus and commitment to get a long-term return on investment.
- Hype is a sign that something is broadly used. Guerrillas look for opportunities to have the first-mover advantage rather than following the herd.

You can protect yourself from the hype by

- watching other guerrillas and innovators that cater to your target market. What is their feedback in relation to the new technology or tool?
- looking for hard data on the tool, product, or technology. Get your data from multiple sources to confirm their accuracy. Forrester Research, MarketingProfs.com, or your local chapter of the Social Media Club are great places to find accurate information.
- checking the credibility of those who claim to be having success with the technology. Are they profitable? Is what they are doing sustainable and scalable?
- remembering that a good marketing attack takes months or even years to be fully effective. Be careful about jumping from idea to idea without allowing ideas time to mature. The latest thing may not be the most effective thing for your business.

2. Curiosity

Sir Alexander Fleming of Scotland discovered penicillin serendipitously. He was observing staphylococcus and looking for a way to battle this bacteria without harming people's immune system. A not-so-organized Fleming had petri dishes unwashed and stacked in the sink. He went away on a brief trip. During this time several mold cultures grew in and around some of the petri dishes. Somehow the mold and the staphylococcus were mixed by accident, and Fleming discovered that this fungus was able to kill the bacteria. This serendipitous event lead to the discovery of penicillin and has now saved what is likely millions of lives. Mr. Fleming was constantly trying new things and asking "why?" and "what if?"

Guerrillas aren't afraid to experiment, make mistakes, or try new things to gain a competitive advantage. Not unlike Alexander Fleming, guerrillas need to be willing to combine different elements of marketing and strategy in a creative fashion. They then need to be curious when new and exciting or even unexpected results arise. They also investigate, measure, and document the results so they can replicate the results on a grand scale.

Some "what if?" and "I wonder" questions that a curious guerrilla could ask are:

- → What if I started giving more reports away for free online?
- → What if I blogged five times a week and decreased my length of entry to no more than 200 words?
- → I wonder what would happen if I asked Guy Kawasaki to do a guest blog on our site?
- → I wonder if I had my podcasts transcribed and posted in my blog if it would increase reader retention?
- → What if I asked my readers to contribute content to our blog and rewarded them for doing so?
- → I wonder why fewer people blog on the weekends? Is there an opportunity in this?

Chris Anderson, author of *Free: The Future of a Radical Price* (Hyperion, 2009), asked "What if I gave 144,000 copies of my book away for free online?" The answer for him was a rapid and sustained *New York Times* and Amazon.com bestseller status.

3. The Ability to Sprint

There will be small windows of opportunity, and the guerrilla is always ready to exploit them with energy, passion, and resources. The world and the internet move very fast. Sometimes marketing and business opportunities come quickly. Being at the right place and the right time is only one part of the formula. Being prepared and ready to take advantage of these opportunities is the magic ingredient in the formula for success.

Some things to help you be ready to sprint are:

- Having a plan in place and a team ready in the event that one of your marketing attacks goes viral; make sure your business is scalable for increased demand.
- Being prepared to pull a 24-hour shift or a 14-day work shift when a huge opportunity hits. Once you have momentum, capitalize on it. Things will eventually slow down, and you can rest then.
- Being ready if things go bad in your social media. Sometimes sprinting is about quickly and aggressively dealing with an onslaught of negative feedback or news. Taking 24 hours, or even two hours, to respond to customer complaints or competitive slander is too long. You need to be ready to respond immediately and stomp out those brand-burning fires.

4. The Ability to Run Marathons

Many battles are battles of attrition. Guerrillas know how to wear their competition down and build a presence through consistency.

One of the biggest costs in marketing is not running bad campaigns or promotions, it's quitting on good campaigns and marketing attacks too soon. The ability to run marathons has many aspects. Guerrillas must

- → have a long-term plan that goes beyond a monthly or quarterly focus.
- → have a marketing calendar that they follow daily.
- → be focused on business goals, not distracted or enamored by the latest technology.
- → understand that a customer may need to be exposed to a message 27 times before brand recognition starts. Frequency and adding value will win hearts, mindshare, and therefore walletshare over time.
- → understand that when a social media technology becomes familiar, it's easy to become bored with it and move on to the next thing. You will be the first person to tire of your blog, Twitter activity, or Google Buzz account. Exciting and effective aren't always synonymous. Focus on what works and what is profitable, and don't worry about the cool factor that most early adopters fall victim to.

5. Transparent

Guerrillas know that truth, empathy, and integrity are keys to social media marketing, and they build trust and loyalty through transparency. In the past we could live dual lives as marketers, CEOs, and even citizens. Today we are on stage 24 hours a day. Everyone is armed with a smartphone, video capture devices, and the ability to post information about us and what we are up to.

Guerrilla social media marketers must be transparent, open, and community focused. Today trust and credibility are our currencies, especially in regards to those we are connected to in social networks and communities online.

Guerrilla Transparency Means

- → thinking before we post content online. Make sure it's true and accurate—people will find any untruths or half-truths, often immediately.

- → being open about business practices and policies. Don't hide behind the fine print in your customer agreements. Customers no longer tell 11 friends when they feel they have been mislead—they tell their 10,000 Twitter friends. Secrecy and legal cleverness can become brand killers.

- → being your true self. Guerrillas know that people buy from people. They want an emotional and personal connection with their suppliers and business connections. They allow their true colors and personality to shine online. If that's not a pretty prospect and they have things to work on, true guerrillas work on who they are and improve their leadership capacity.

6. Community Focused

A guerrilla builds, connects, and helps the community. Within that community are other guerrilla allies who will become assets. Social media marketing is 90 percent community, contribution, and connection. Ten percent is about targeted, relevant marketing to people who want and need what you have to offer NOW. By contributing great content and by helping customers and members of the community achieve their dreams and goals, we can in turn become successful.

Think "what's in it for me?" from your target market's perspective.

If you're new to social media or have just joined a new social network, take your time. Guerrillas get to know a community. They want to determine what the community's values and etiquette are, and they also make a concerted effort to identify the key influencers in that community.

After getting in sync with the community, the goal is to become noticed and build your brand through contribution and value. This can come in many forms, but some common ways this can be done are by

- finding influencers in the community and helping them promote a project, product, or cause they are connected to.
- providing value-added content such as white papers, studies, tips, free webinars, podcasts, or other business or personal development tools.
- providing opportunities for other people in the community to connect, collaborate, or do business with each other.
- introducing more people to the network or community.

After we have connected with the community, built rapport, and really developed an understanding of the distinct needs, values, and preferences of the group, we can then plan and launch a relevant, focused, on-target guerrilla marketing attack. Too many marketers skip the community-building stage and jump right into blasting marketing messages off to audiences that are unreceptive. Guerrillas value and understand community. They take time to really understand and connect with their market.

7. Profit Driven

Guerrilla marketing measures success by profits, not clicks, visitors, or any cool factor. Many people mistake popularity for profitability. There are a lot of bloggers, Twitter celebrities, and YouTube video moguls who will wow people with their 30,000 followers, 10,000 blog subscribers, or 50,000 video views. These are important and exciting statistics, but they mean very little unless they create profit or a net positive action. These subscribers, friends, or views have to eventually turn into something. Many companies boast about their revenues. Far fewer boast about profit, and profit is what guerrilla marketing is all about.

There are many self-proclaimed experts in social media out there who will show you how to get lots of followers, fans, and subscribers. Be wary of these promises. You must value your time and effort, and measure your success in terms of profit, not gross sales or the fact that you are seen as cool or popular.

Guerrillas also use new media technologies to reduce fixed costs and automate business processes. Fancy offices, expensive parking spaces, and nice addresses are hallmarks of things that used to signify success. Successful people used to also boast about how busy they were. Guerrillas know that today it's about maximizing success while minimizing the impact on our time and overall costs. They are constantly looking for ways to produce a high-quality product or service while automating, outsourcing, or delegating costly activities that impact their most valuable asset—time.

8. Tech Hungry

Technology is the guerrilla social media marketer's core weapon and competency. Guerrillas are always learning more about technology. Today's world of business has no place for technophobes. Technophobia will be the demise of many companies and industries over the next decade. It is absolutely necessary to immerse yourself fully into all things tech and study it like your life depends on it. Understanding technology and all of its applications to business better and sooner than their competitors is vital.

Always be asking "where are we going? What is the next Twitter or Facebook going to be?"

Tips for Becoming a Guerrilla Geek

→ Join Meetup.com and look for groups that get together and share information on emerging trends and technology. Many major cities have an abundance of these groups. Some that you may want to join are:

1. *Blogger meetups.* Bloggers share information on the latest blogging tools, applications, automation techniques, traffic building strategies, and best practices for creating content.

2. *Flickr and photography meetups.* These groups discuss almost everything you need to know about digital photography and image-capture devices.

3. *Apple and Mac meetups.* Apple makes some of the top social media tech tools. These are great groups to help you ramp up quickly with all the uses for Apple products in social media.

4. *Video meetups.* These groups usually focus on best practices in shooting video, producing video, editing, and even distribution and marketing.

5. *Internet marketing and search engine marketing meetups.* These groups discuss and share insights on everything from ranking well on Google to effective shopping cart design.

6. *New media marketing meetups.* Most cities have more than one of these groups. They are great places to meet other guerrillas and share best practices in social media marketing.

➤ Join your local Social Media Club (the world's largest social media association). It was founded by Chris Heuer in July 2006. He started Social Media Club in order to help professionalize the industry and share best practices and ethical issues surrounding social media. One of its other core mandates is to expand media literacy globally.

➤ Devote time each day to reading blogs and listening to podcasts about technology and global business trends. Some great blogs and resources online include:

1. *Technorati.* This site rates and indexes the top blogs on the internet. Its tech category lists the most popular and current tech news from thousands of blogs on the internet.

2. *PostRank.com*. This site rates blogs by engagement score, taking into account comments, tweets, links, and social bookmarking to rank how engaged people are with the blog. It lists the top social media and technology blogs and updates their rankings by the day.

3. *iTunes*. There are literally dozens of high quality podcasts (audio downloads) on iTunes. You will need to download their software for your PC or Mac. Once loaded up, click on the iTunes store button and then click on podcasts. You can search by keyword or browse by category. You will be able to find and subscribe to dozens of free tech podcasts.

4. *Read* Wired *magazine*. *Wired* has both a network of blogs and a print magazine. They cover everything from mainstream tech trends to off-the-wall inventions. They are a great source for new ideas, trends, and insights.

➤ Attend social media and tech gadget conferences. Attending seminars and rubbing elbows with bonafide social media geeks can help reduce your learning curve. You can often pick up tips, tricks, and insights in a much shorter time than you would by digging for the information online.

➤ Start associating with people who have good tech knowledge. They don't necessarily have to be guerrillas; it would be your job to take the tech insight you learn from them and apply guerrilla principles to the knowledge. Peer mentoring and learning through modeling successful or knowledgeable people is vital. Observe, listen, and watch what these people do.

➤ Follow and connect with people who are in the tech space on Twitter, Facebook, LinkedIn, Google Buzz, and any other platform you can find them on. Often they will tweet or post status updates about new and exciting technology, and even provide insight into great blogs, conferences, and resources.

9. Self-Developer

Guerrillas know that technology and business move fast. They are constantly learning more to stay ahead of the competition. Because social media makes us highly visible, our actions, business strategy, and innovation will attract a lot of emulators. Our customers and prospects online are also constantly evolving in how they use the social web. We need to constantly be learning and looking for trends and changes in how technology is being used.

We cannot afford to wait for our human resource department to hold a training seminar. We often can't wait for industry experts to compile all of the data we need to make the perfect decision. Guerrillas seeking to maintain a competitive lead must learn, research, experiment, and innovate on the fly.

Einstein was arguably the most accomplished self-developer of the 20th century. He would set a large goal or objective, something that many others wouldn't dare to even hypothesize about. Then he would work diligently toward proving his theory. When he would get stuck or got out of his depth of knowledge, he would inventory what specialized knowledge and insight he would need and then totally commit himself to mastering the concept. His ability to completely focus on learning a new competency or field of science quickly and in great depth is what made him a master.

Guerrillas often start with a big goal, a plan, and only part of the resources they need to reach that goal. When they get stuck or come across the challenge, they don't back off or try an easier route. They inventory what they need to learn or discover to take the next step, and they intensely focus on that competency until they master it. Sometimes it means partnering with other guerrillas, but many times when you're breaking new ground in the social media space, you will need to innovate and experiment with new approaches and disciplines. Being a self-developer means we can evolve at a rate much faster than the rest of the marketplace.

10. Leadership Mentality

Guerrillas observe the community and gather intelligence, but they are always thinking about what is next. They create trends, unique solutions, and are thought leaders.

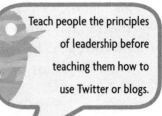

Teach people the principles of leadership before teaching them how to use Twitter or blogs.

THINK LEADERSHIP AND ENGAGEMENT VS. BRANDING AND PITCHING

The term "social media marketing" is misleading. It is often seen as a tool or tactic. A lot of people mistakenly see social media and social networks as distribution channels for their clever marketing and branding campaigns. This is only one layer of social media. Social media is more a leadership game than a marketing game. Our branding and trust building, which are key elements in any sales or marketing process, come from conversations about and with our company or product.

From an online marketing perspective, leadership is about engagement. Engagement isn't just about having conversations with our customers. It is also not just about listening to the marketplace and responding to it. Engagement is about making the customer and the community feel genuinely listened to. Each conversation, interaction, or marketing tactic must somehow add value, entertain, or inform people. It's about making people's lives, businesses, and community a little better with each interaction.

Our marketing reach and effectiveness will rise and fall with our capacity to lead and engage. This is why sustained effort and consistency are so vital. Anyone with a hefty marketing budget and a good e-mail list can get people to join a group or online social network. There are thousands of online communities out there that are ghost towns. Their founders were able get the initial buy-in, but many forgot an important factor. Customers will go where they are invited, but they will stay only if they are engaged consistently. Building a social network, a fan base, or community hub is only step one. Guerrillas know they must consistently provide new opportunities, insights, dialogue, and inspiration to those who are connected to them online.

Herein lies the big question: do you possess the ten personality traits of a guerrilla social media marketer? If not, are you willing to do the work and go through the positive change necessary to be successful? If your answer is yes to either of these questions, then we would like to officially welcome you to the guerrilla family of marketers and leaders.

The reality is that it's almost impossible to be strong in all ten traits. Most guerrillas will have five to seven areas of strength. They will offset their weaknesses by hiring or collaborating with people who possess those missing personality traits. The key is to identify what we are good at naturally and turn it into a strength, then develop a plan to mitigate the risks associated with the traits we lack.

Figure 1.1 is a self-assessment to help you identify which personality traits you possess and which ones you will need to develop.

FIGURE 1.1

Evaluating Personality Traits

Rate yourself from 1 to 10, 1 being you don't possess this trait at all and 10 being that you fully embody this trait in your daily business and marketing activities:

1. Immune to hype: I search for truth, verify information, and execute with dependable tools and strategies. I don't get caught up in unfounded hype.	Score /10
Action steps required:	

FIGURE 1.1

Evaluating Personality Traits, continued

2. Curiosity: I'm not afraid to experiment, make mistakes, or try new things to gain a competitive advantage.	Score /10
Action steps required:	
3. The ability to sprint: I am always ready to exploit small windows of opportunity with all of my energy, passion, and resources.	Score /10
Action steps required:	
4. The ability to run marathons: I know how to wear my competition down and build a presence through consistency.	Score /10
Action steps required:	
5. Transparent: I know that truth, empathy, and integrity are keys to social media marketing, and I build trust and loyalty through transparency.	Score /10
Action steps required:	
6. Community focused: I build, connect, and help the community. Within that community are other guerrilla allies with whom I align and collaborate.	Score /10
Action steps required:	
7. Profit driven: I measure success by profits, not clicks, visitors, or any "cool factor."	Score /10
Action steps required:	
8. Tech hungry: Technology is my core weapon and competency. I am always learning more about technology.	Score /10
Action steps required:	

FIGURE 1.1

Evaluating Personality Traits, continued

9. Self-developer: I know that technology and business move fast. I am constantly learning more to stay ahead of the competition.	Score /10
Action steps required:	
10. Leadership mentality: I observe the community, gather intelligence, and am always thinking about what is next. I create trends and unique solutions, and am considered a leader by many.	Score /10
Action steps required:	

CHAPTER 2

BUILDING THE GUERRILLA'S PERSONAL BRAND

People define a brand as a logo, a feeling, a name, or even a promise. Guerrilla social media marketers understand that a brand is whatever the customer thinks it is. To have a positive, memorable, and inspiring brand in social media, we must represent an idea, meme, or set of values that people want to talk about and share.

Twitter users produce over a billion Twitter updates per month; YouTube shows billions of hours of video in the same period. Combine that with

19

> Evaluate your strategy as if you were looking through your customers' eyes. Ask "So What?" a lot.

traditional media messages on television, radio, print, and e-mail, and today's marketplace is being bombarded with messages and updates so fast that consumers can feel lost and overwhelmed. They look for people and organizations that they can trust to help guide them in this sea of noise. Your personal and corporate brand must be a trustworthy beacon in the marketplace if you are to succeed.

GUERRILLAS REALIZE THAT EVERYONE IS NOW IN THE MEDIA BUSINESS

In years gone by, individuals and companies could live a life of duplicity. Big companies could operate unethically and without regard for others and still manage to buy themselves a squeaky clean image. There were fewer media outlets. Companies could buy inventory, shout loud enough about their brand, and convince consumers of almost anything. There were only a handful of TV channels and a limited number of journalists to chase down stories. Even good stories could end up on the cutting room floor of newsrooms for a variety of reasons.

Today there are an unlimited number of media outlets. Everyone is his or her own media company. Many people have smartphones, and those phones have mobile internet access, video, a camera, and audio recording devices. Whether we like it or not, we are all on stage all of the time; anyone can snap a picture, record a video, or post a Tweet online about our brand. Nothing ends up on the cutting room floor anymore. From the mundane act to the bizarre, they're almost all recorded and uploaded to the web by the hundreds of individuals you walk by, see, and interact with daily.

At any point a customer interacts with a company, there is an opportunity to have a positive or negative branding experience. At that interaction point, armed with their smartphone, camera, or video recorder, they will also have an opportunity to impact the brand. In seconds they will tell the world the truth or just their opinion of what you are really about. We can no longer claim to be one thing in public and another in private; with one click or one Tweet, the world can see our true brand identity.

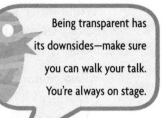

Being transparent has its downsides—make sure you can walk your talk. You're always on stage.

GUERRILLA BRANDS ARE AUTHENTIC

With all of the noise and so much less-than-authentic marketing in the marketplace, there are opportunities out there for guerrillas. The opportunity lies in providing a distinct, authentic, and transparent brand that people can trust.

What Is an Authentic Guerrilla Brand?

- ➤ It makes promises and statements that can be backed up today, tomorrow, and indefinitely.
- ➤ It is customer-focused and sells and markets to the customer what he needs and wants.
- ➤ It is consistent, 24 hours a day, 365 days a year, in any geography or language.
- ➤ It doesn't take shortcuts for short-term gain; the guerrilla brand builds customers for life.
- ➤ It is, however, fallible. All brands have imperfections and weaknesses, and a guerrilla brand does not shovel these under the rug. It takes feedback and improves the customer experience.
- ➤ It is accessible. No executives are in an ivory tower; no labyrinths have been built to keep out the unhappy customer.
- ➤ It is focused on a distinct area of true competency and expertise, and that is why people gravitate to the guerrilla brand.

Beyond being authentic there are several other important characteristics that your brand must have to succeed in the social media space. Guerrilla social media brands are:

- Easy to understand
- Distinct
- Easy to share
- Easy to find
- Always on
- Human
- Consistent across all platforms and media

GUERRILLA BRANDS
ARE EASY TO UNDERSTAND

When describing their business to people, guerrilla brands are easy to understand, and it is obvious what their benefits are to their target audience. An effective, short business description is an effective way of ensuring your brand is easy to understand.

The 140-Character Business Description

The goal here is to develop a description of what you do in 140 characters (approximately 18 words) or less. It should also be void of all acronyms or jargon that may confuse your prospect. This description can be used to answer a customer question on a social network. It could be a tagline on a video, or you can use it in-person at an industry event.

Here are a few examples submitted to us via Twitter from real guerrillas:

- "I help people achieve their real estate goals to purchase or sell property with my experience, knowledge, and connections!" —Jackie MacDonald (@listingproperty)

- ➤ "We are wealth protection specialists offering our clients peace of mind with the best insurance products on the market." — Desirée Dupuis (@threesixtyfg)
- ➤ "Marketing Vancouver's condominiums 100 percent digitally, transparently, innovatively & powerfully, beyond the industry standard." —Ian Watt (@ianwatt)
- ➤ "Chill Monkeys Apparel makes stylish clothes for cool little boys." —Alexis Hind (@AlexisHind)
- ➤ "Mortgage consulting services that allow you to own your own home with dollars left over to live the life you want to live." —Jason Krist (@MortgageNurse)
- ➤ "Helping Realtors build the business they desire, so they can live the life they deserve." —Darin Persinger (@DarinPersinger)
- ➤ "We help make complicated IT systems simple and help small business leverage technology to be productive and grow!" —Sarah Morton (@sarahmortonvan)

What is your 140-character business description? Make sure it tells the prospect what you do and how it helps them. Try it:

_____

_____

This is not something you would post to Twitter as a general update or say the very moment you meet someone. It often follows the question that most people ask after they get to know you: "What do you do?"

Once You Have Consent, Deepen the Conversation

After you have answered the question of what you want to do succinctly and in a way that provokes curiosity and interest, you can expand upon what you do in more detail. Online you have multiple media in all different formats to expand upon what you do. You can also move interested prospects into webinars, Skype chat or Skype video, or even meet them offline.

The key is to be producing content in multiple formats consistently. This content can then be shared after an initial conversation to increase the prospect's knowledge about your business. Because people absorb information differently, have your business information and brand story in multiple formats. This information can come in many forms:

- White papers or case studies in PDF format
- Customer testimonials
- A list of customer Tweets and endorsements in the form of a blog entry
- Podcasts (downloadable MP3/audio files)
- Product or service demonstrations in video format
- In-depth downloadable digital brochures for people who like detail
- Brief 200-word pages, blog posts, or downloadable sheets for people who like the big picture
- Live chat with you or your customer service team
- Forums and Facebook pages for customers and prospects to share information about you

Guerrillas know that their business idea and value must be easy to understand. They also know that not all people learn the same way so they provide information in multiple formats from multiple perspectives, which help tell their brand story.

DISTINCT

Your brand, benefits, and messaging have to be distinct. Social media platforms and communities are full of noise; contrast helps you be the clear signal amongst the chatter. Distinctiveness comes in many forms.

Your Logo

Your logo must be distinctive and simple. Avoid universal images that make the prospect say "That looks just like XYZ's logo" because you will quickly be grouped with everyone else and forgotten. It must also have multimedia applicability. In other words, it should look great on a billboard, on a website icon, shrunk for a business card, or on a video. Unless you're in the graphic design business, it is advisable that you invest in the services of a professional design firm or an individual designer. Seek out brands in your local community that have distinct logos and find out who did the design for them.

Frequency and Depth of Content

If everyone else blogs every two to three days, blog every day. If their videos are on average three minutes long, make yours one minute long or 20 minutes long. If their blog entries are published in the morning, post yours in the afternoon. If your competitors produce five-minute teaser podcasts three times a week, produce 15-minute podcasts five days a week.

Media

Much like the tempo of the rest of the marketplace, your media must also be distinct or differentiated. If everyone in your community is using blogs and squeeze pages as a means of capturing leads or communicating what they do, you may want to look at video blogging, webinars, podcasts, or any other medium that they're not using.

As an added note, get better at using various types of media than your competitors. Know all of the applications and methods of producing content in an effective way. Once you choose your guerrilla social media marketing weapons, as we discuss in an upcoming chapter, master those tools and get better and more knowledgeable than anyone else in your space.

Format or Style

Another way to be distinct is to produce content in a different format or style than your competition. It's important that this style reflects your organizational values and brand, but it also has to be innovative and creative enough to make it memorable.

You may find that your competitors are spending days or even weeks producing slick high-definition videos in a studio. In this case you may want to grab an easy-to-use lower-resolution video camera and record in a guy-on-the-street raw video format. The key is to use a format that stands above the sea of content that is out there. Then stick with that format. Over time, you will own this style in the minds of your market.

You can also vary the formats of your website, your blog and blog entries, or the type of photos you publish. Even the introduction of a podcast and how you introduce your guests can be a point of distinction.

Level of Interaction

Guerrillas know that social media and social networks are bi-directional communications tools. Most of your competitors will be stingy with their real level of interaction and conversations with the marketplace. Chat more, contribute more, and listen more than your competitors. See Figure 2.1 for some ways to do this.

Context of Benefits

Everyone seems to explain benefits the same way. People talk about saving money, time, helping you go faster, and making money easily. You know the drill. Prospects immediately delete these common terms mentally, looking for a differentiator. As an example, don't

FIGURE 2.1

Differentiate Your Customer Interaction

Traditional Marketers Say	Guerrillas Know
Being conversational doesn't scale.	Positive conversations can go viral via online word of mouth and grow your brand geometrically.
You should find a way to automate your interaction and responses.	Taking the time to personally tailor our messages and communications creates rapport and trust in our brand. Trust in your brand means business.
Broadcast messages across multiple channels; it's a numbers game.	Listening to multiple communities online can help you respond with the right message to the right prospect at the right time. It means you don't waste money and time or create noise.
Tease the market with free reports, meager discounts, and mass appeal offers.	Giving real value, truly customized solutions, and things that will help your market creates loyalty and a desire to reciprocate and do business with you.
If you don't get a return on investment from a community or target market, move on quickly and find a more receptive market.	It takes many conversations and value-added interactions to gain the trust, loyalty, and mindshare of a community. Having ongoing dialogue and involvement with your connections is what it takes to make a guerrilla marketing attack fully pay. Investing long term in the right market is always a good strategy.

just save people time—help them spend more time with their family or doing their favorite sport.

If everyone else is talking about helping people lose weight faster, talk about helping people lose weight scientifically and permanently. Make your benefits distinct, more detailed, and more tailored to your target market. Your benefits should talk directly to the needs of your customer and prospect. But having benefits is not enough. What's even better than benefits? Solutions to problems. Offer them. You must stand out.

Your Personal Leadership Style

If you are a team of one or lead a corporate team of 1,000, your personal leadership style can impact and differentiate your brand. When someone talks about Apple, they cannot avoid thinking about Steve Jobs. His leadership style, the way he interacts, and his values help form the emotional connection people have with the brand. Tony Hsieh of Zappos has a leadership style that is more engaging than any other online retailer of his company's size. Tony takes the time to interact on Twitter with average customers and also shows up at events and conventions to directly engage with the public. That's the most social of all the social media. The accessibility and transparency—Tony creates those through his ongoing blogging. Tweeting and in-person meetings help him personalize and humanize the Zappos brand. This is a point of distinctiveness for Zappos. As the founder or CEO of an organization that has committed to the guerrilla way, being more transparent, accessible, and responsive to your market gives your entire organization a core area of differentiation.

Your Staff and Team Brand Personalities

Guerrillas know that every person in their organization is part of their brand. A brand is a promise, and each interaction with anyone in your organization either delivers or fails to deliver on that promise. This means that everyone in the organization is recruited, trained, and mentored to resonate with the brand and organizational values. This also means that everyone from the marketing department to the front desk reception is trained in the rules, tools, and principles of guerrilla social media marketing.

EASY TO SHARE

If you have an easy-to-understand message that is distinct, people will want to share it. Guerrillas make it easy for people to share information and ideas using social technologies.

Many great videos never go viral online. Why? They are often embedded on websites in ways that makes them almost impossible to post and share with other people. Many blog entries are also not shared because the blogger has failed to add one-click social bookmarking functionality to his pages. Many shopping cart pages on e-commerce sites don't have their fantastic offers shared for the same reason. This is due to lack of foresight or just plain laziness.

> The easier it is for people to share your great content, the more viral your marketing will become. Integrate your content with all major social bookmarking sites and social media networks to maximize your reach.

If you're going to post photos, make multiple versions in different resolutions available. Don't make journalists dig for your e-mail to request a high-resolution photo or your personal or corporate bio. Make it easy for them to contact and spread the word about you. Don't make it difficult or onerous for your customers to share your information with their friends. Every page of your website, blog, forum, or social networking portal should be able to be shared with one click. When you make people work too hard to share your great information, you miss the true viral marketing opportunity in social media and social networks.

EASY TO FIND

When people want your help or want access to your ideas or resources, they need to be able to find you easily. Guerrillas make their businesses easily accessible. There are several ways you need to be easy to find:

- → *Via the telephone.* People must be able to quickly connect with you when they want to do business. Make sure your number is easy to find on all websites, blogs, e-mail signatures, Twitter profiles, Facebook pages, and any other destination you have. If you feel that you don't want to directly interact with unqualified customers via telephone, hire someone or outsource it, but make this option available to customers who prefer to connect via telephone.

- → *Your website resources.* Have an easy-to-navigate website with a well laid out and intuitive sitemap. Also have a "search this site" box that allows your customer to search your site like a database. The more time they spend hunting and poking around the less they will stick around.

People want results and answers fast. They tire quickly and leave your website or blog if your content is not well organized and searchable.

- → *Search engine optimization.* The art of getting found on Google, Bing, or other search engines is indeed an important discipline. Make sure your website is designed well and uses site software that search engines find easy to index and crawl. Take your time researching what your market searches for and make sure that your site title tags, descriptions, page names, and text are optimized for both human eyes and the Google bots. Those bots will impact whether or not you are found when someone searches for you or your product.

➤ *Social networks.* Reserve your name and your company's name on every social network and social media space out there. You may not use all of them actively, but guerrillas know that they should be where their customers are. If a customer searches for you in LinkedIn, Facebook, Google Buzz, Twitter, Xing, or any of the other major networks, they should be able to find you quickly and connect with you.

You may be an awesome blogger, but does the world know? Search engine optimization, social networks, and offline promotions are needed.

➤ *Local search.* Many of the search engines and location-based social networks allow you to set up geographically specific profiles. Make sure your business is registered in each locality where you are doing business. Start with Google Local, but also make sure you register your business on sites like FourSquare, your local Yellow Page directory, and even regional Twitter directories like Twellow.com. Make it simple to find you locally.

ALWAYS ON

Almost everyone has a telephone with a camera and video capture device built in. A guerrilla social media marketer uses this as a branding opportunity and also manages the risks associated with this.

Being always on means being aware and ready to capture life's moments instantly. Have something to take notes, take photos, record video, and record audio on you at all times. Just when you least expect it, you could record an amazing customer testimonial or have a flash of insight that you want to share with your tribe or community. Many times if we wait for the next day or week to post this information it loses its impact. General George Patton said, "A pretty good plan executed today is better than a perfect plan being executed tomorrow."

Being always on also means using tools that make it easy to publish content to the web. Too often, people invest in gear that is expensive and requires a lot of knowledge and technical ability to go from content creation to content publishing. While the pro is at home digitally enhancing the pictures they took, their amateur guerrilla competitor has already posted their own pictures from their smartphone and has now moved on to the next big event or marketing opportunity.

Being always on is also about understanding that at any moment you may have an opportunity to have others record, photograph, or blog about you. Your activities in public always have to be consistent with your brand promise. This also means you need your business description and marketing tools and resources ready at any time you may be required to share and use them.

BEING HUMAN

The world is now known to be flat, transparent, and very personal. The guerrilla's brand is built upon very human characteristics and personable intimate commerce. Being human means not automating anything that creates an intimate close bond with the customer. It also requires that you share more of your opinions, hobbies, and life than you have previously.

Engagement is not just about listening; it's about empathy, rapport, and making people feel heard.

As we have mentioned, people buy from people. They believe their friends more than they believe polished, sanitized brands and advertisements. Because they believe their friends, you must become their friend by finding common ground. This could come in the form of their realizing that they have the same interest in golfing as the CEO because they read a Tweet about the CEO's last golfing trip. Being human is about being willing to have more personal, real, authentic conversations than typical executives, marketers, or companies do in the marketplace. It's also about spending more time listening and empathizing with your customers. Some people call it engagement. Engagement isn't just about listening; it's about making the customer feel totally heard and listened to.

Engagement is the goal; social media are the tools.

CONSISTENT ACROSS PLATFORMS AND MEDIA

Let's step into the prospect's perspective. He's online reading fantastic blog entries, watching videos, and interacting with a boutique ad agency. He has even visited the agency's Facebook page to chat with other customers about the agency's work. Overall the agency has been able to present a professional, trendy, detail-orientated, and creative brand image to the prospect.

The prospect then calls the agency. When the phone is answered, John, the founder, simply says, "Ah . . . Hello?" After a bit of dialogue they agree to meet, and John is invited into their office. When John arrives, he is late. He's wearing a poorly fitting sports jacket, scuffed conservative-looking shoes, and outdated spectacles. Throughout the conversation John asks basic questions about the prospect's business that can be found on the company website and talks about typical traditional marketing ideas for its business. At the end of the meeting, John leaves the prospect a business card with a logo that has a completely different color scheme than the one on John's website. The meeting was pleasant. After all, John is obviously a nice guy, but John never got a call back. John was incongruent with his online brand efforts, both in his very untrendy and unkempt appearance and his unresearched and traditional approach to marketing. His prospect was looking for a trendy, creative, and detail-orientated agency.

> Consistency, conviction, passion, and focus are needed to see a social media plan succeed.

Many social media marketers spend too many hours just focusing on their social media presence and brand, and hiding behind their computer screen. What they forget is that the most successful marketers use an integrated marketing approach. It's not enough to just write good blog entries or create great landing pages or videos. All of your media and interactions must consistently deliver your brand promise. This consistency creates a sense of security and trust for the prospect, customer, community, and your own staff.

In the updated fourth edition of *Guerrilla Marketing* (Mariner Books, 2007), there are over 200 guerrilla marketing weapons listed. In this book you will learn about another 150 guerrilla social media marketing weapons. Your tone, brand representation, personal appearance, behavior, and customer engagement philosophy must be applied consistently across the assortment of guerrilla marketing weapons you choose to use.

The worksheet in Figure 2.2 reflects on how well your brand embodies the core characteristics of a guerrilla brand.

FIGURE 2.2

Core Characteristics of a Guerrilla Brand

Rate your brand from 1 to 10: 1 means your brand does not possess this characteristic at all, 10 that your brand consistently and effectively embodies this characteristic.

1. Easy to understand: When describing your business to people, your description is easy to understand, and it is obvious what the benefits are to your target audience.	Score ___/10
Action steps required:	
2. Distinct: Your brand, benefits, and messaging are distinct. Social media platforms and communities are full of noise and contrast; you are unique and stand out from the crowd.	Score ___/10
Action steps required:	
3. Easy to share: You make it easy for people to share information and ideas using social technologies.	Score ___/10
Action steps required:	
4. Easy to find: When people want your help or want access to your ideas or resources, they are able to find you easily. You make your business easy to find.	Score ___/10
Action steps required:	
5. Always on: It seems that nearly everyone has a telephone with a camera and video capture device built in. You use this as a branding opportunity and also manage the risks associated with this.	Score ___/10
Action steps required:	

FIGURE 2.2

Core Characteristics of a Guerrilla Brand, continued

6. Being human: Your brand is built upon very human characteristics and personable intimate commerce.	Score ___/10
Action steps required:	
7. Consistent branding across platforms and media: You ensure that all print, web, and other media that you use have consistent messaging and brand styling. Your face-to-face interactions are also consistent with the brand in dress, behavior, and daily actions.	Score ___/10
Action steps required:	

CHAPTER 3

THE TOP TEN ATTRIBUTES OF A GUERRILLA SOCIAL MEDIA MARKETER

 With a strong guerrilla brand, we can build or develop the other core attributes of a guerrilla social media marketer. These ten attributes are really just the beginning. There are many other insights, attitudes, and attributes you will need to acquire and develop on your guerrilla path. These top ten attributes of a guerrilla social media marketer are:

1. Name

2. Strong ongoing branding strategy

3. Positioning through listening and dialogue

4. Quality

5. Distribution
6. Free and variable
7. Referral and rewards program
8. Likeability
9. Testimonials
10. Reputation

1. NAME

Your name will be used for domain names, for social network profiles, on name badges, and even at social functions. Your name should be easily remembered, timeless, and cross cultures and languages with ease. More specifically, your name should:

➤ *Be distinctive*. It should not be easily confused with your competitors or other businesses in the marketplace. Too many people choose business names or domain names that are so generic that they are easily confused with competitors or buried along with similarly named businesses in the Google index.

➤ *Immediately create interest* in what you do or spur a sense of curiosity. This interest must be reinforced and increased with every exposure to your business name. This means it must not be based upon a short-term trend but something that can be representative of your company even as your customers and organization evolve over time.

➤ *Be hard or impossible to duplicate*. Your competitors will try to capitalize on your hard work online by choosing domain names and social IDs that are similar to yours. They do this in hopes that your customers and prospects will be directed to their sites and offers. Your name should be so unique that if competitors attempt to copy it, the act will be glaringly obvious and do damage to their brand. As a further step, trademark your name if at all possible. Then reserve all major domain names and variations of your domains and social network IDs.

➤ *Be easy to pronounce and remember in any language or region you do or might do business in.* Do a search of the name you are choosing in those regions. Don't just search the literal spelling; also consult with a local who speaks the language to see if your business name phonetically sounds like something else in their language or region.

Your name should not:

➤ *Be safe.* Being safe means fitting into a sea of other marketers who are taking it safe, which only guarantees that you be compared to or grouped into a large list of potential suppliers. You need to stand out.

➤ *Appeal to the whole world.* Your name should actually help qualify the right prospects and repel those that don't resonate with your organizational values and brand focus. People remember brands that don't play it safe but declare what they represent. Don't try to appeal to the whole world.

➤ *Be in the form of an acronym.* For every IBM there are thousands of three- and four-letter acronym-formatted names that are mistaken, remembered incorrectly, or forgotten almost immediately. Your business or product name should tell people what you do or imply how it could benefit your prospective client. Some people say that a picture is worth a thousand words, but the right company name can paint a picture, evoke emotions, and create impressions about your brand.

2. STRONG ONGOING BRANDING STRATEGY

As stated earlier we must have a recognizable brand that is easy to share and gets above the noise. Guerrilla social media marketers are always branding and protecting their brands.

Your Branding Must Be Consistent and Long Term

Guerrillas know that brands are living, growing, dynamic organisms. They have a personality and promise attached to them. They're not static. Today's brands are formed based upon the ongoing exposure and interaction they have with customers and prospects.

It will take many months, and most likely years, before a brand is well established in the minds and hearts of the marketplace. Many entrepreneurs and marketers second-guess their brand and the interest level of their target market. They quit and try a new approach and shift their positioning, hoping that in the short term they can get a better result. This constant questioning and second-guessing confuses your customers, prospects, and staff. It also weakens your position against your competitors who are more consistent and confident in their brand.

Have a Plan and Commit to the Plan

Your brand can't just be a casual affair for you and your team. It must be a marriage. Have a well-thought-out, one-year plan complete with marketing calendars, tasks, roles, and responsibilities attached to every aspect. Review and adjust that plan annually; update it, but stay the course. Trust, credibility, and mindshare aren't gained overnight, and once gained they take a continued systematic focus to maintain.

3. POSITIONING THROUGH LISTENING AND DIALOGUE

Traditional marketing says decide on your positioning and build a broadcast marketing plan around that. In social media your customers actually define and own your brand through conversations and user-generated content. Guerrillas create positioning through listening and getting involved in the conversation.

Your brand is a promise; your positioning is the ongoing execution of that promise. Your positioning is the essence of your products, services, and company. It is something that resides in the mind of your customer and is the context through which they see you. Every blog post, video, status update, and forum post you create should be contributing to an overall positioning story about your brand.

A guerrilla positioning story tells your specific niche the following:

- ➤ What your corporate values are and what you represent
- ➤ What you offer and specifically what business you are in
- ➤ What makes you unique, and distinct
- ➤ What you do better than anyone else
- ➤ Who loves to do business with you (your target markets)

Guerrillas Position Through Stories and Conversations

The first step in positioning through social media is to get to know your audience intimately. Commonly referred to as social media monitoring tools, guerrilla intelligence tools allow you to sort through the millions of possible blog posts, Tweets, and videos by honing in on relevant conversations by your target market. Once this target market has been identified and its true needs, wants, communications style, and culture determined, then the conversation begins. It's not a sales pitch; it's a series of questions, value-added content, and engaging conversations using multiple social media. Over time each of these little interactions forms and tells your positioning story. How you answer questions, share information, and produce content must be consistent with your brand and the positioning story you want to tell.

> Not listening to your customer = Brandicide (Brand Homicide). Have a social media listening strategy.

An important thing to note is guerrillas do not manipulate their prospects. They make honest positioning statements, with real-value propositions that appeal to the core needs of their customer.

4. QUALITY

Guerrilla social media marketers represent and/or create only high-quality products, services, and experiences. There's nowhere to hide when things go bad.

Prior to the internet, bad customer service could precipitate into what was known as the 1–11–5 principle. When a customer has a bad unresolved experience, they would on average tell 11 people, who will each will tell 5. This amounts to 67 people who now have a bad impression and poor positioning story to share about the company in question. This would usually happen through one-on-one story-telling, and at most an upset customer might write an easy-to-ignore complaint letter. Today upset customers post those letters on blogs, Twitter, and forums, and create YouTube videos. These posts can last for eternity and erode trust and credibility. As Jeff Bezos, founder of Amazon.com, says, "If you make customers unhappy on the internet, they can each tell 6,000 friends."

When we make that first sale to a customer, it is one of the most expensive things we will ever do. Guerrillas always look at the lifetime value of a customer, and they know that a business that doesn't have a strategy to create repeat purchases is missing out on the majority of the revenue opportunities.

Your customers truly define and position your brand. They define what it is through their conversations and the content they create. Guerrillas know they can influence this branding and positioning by getting involved in the conversation. Defining quality is an extension of this. What matters is what your target market thinks quality is.

Through engaging, listening, observing, and asking for feedback, your customers and prospects will tell you what they feel a quality product, service, or business interaction is. After that, it's the marketer's job to authentically deliver that quality. If we don't deliver quality, social media marketing will only multiply the negative opinion of your brand in the marketplace.

5. DISTRIBUTION

Location! Location! Location! It used to be all about your location. Fancy boardrooms, A-list financial district addresses, expensive furniture, and glass towers. Those were signs of success. Today it's not about having a great office location or business location, it's about having distribution and giving people access to your message and business from anywhere.

The guerilla knows how to be everywhere at once by using social media distribution technologies. The guerrilla marketer is not tied to a desk but is completely mobile and able to do business and take action at any time.

The marketplace is very fragmented. Not all of your customers or markets will be found in one place. Fully engaged guerrillas have a presence on almost every major network and social destination that their customers are on.

The key is to use both technology for distribution and leverage your connections as well. Although we need to be on multiple networks it is inefficient to manually update multiple sites and networks. Marketing weapons like Ping.fm and Hootsuite as well as RSS feed aggregators can help you post a status update once but distribute it to dozens or even hundreds of different social networks. Guerrillas understand and are experts in social media distribution technologies.

The other form of distribution is leveraged distribution of your message through alliances and influencers. Organizations like CNN and NBC get a lot of their breaking news from the front page of Digg.com. Stories that get on the front page of Digg are there because thousands of individuals have voted on the story. What most people don't know is that there are many guerrilla marketing networks made up of Digg users who work together to get stories highly ranked. By forming alliances and agreeing to promote each other's content, their marketing messages can go viral and truly leverage their efforts. Beyond Digg, many successful marketers form blogging, YouTube, Twitter, and Facebook alliances that grow to be very effective and powerful marketing channels.

Working from Anywhere, Anytime

Being able to work from anywhere and publish content when it's fresh and current is vital. Guerrillas design their business so that they are able to unshackle themselves from their office but still stay in constant contact with their team and their customers. This often allows them to live a great lifestyle. They have the freedom to work from anywhere in the world but still get things done. Tools like wikis, VOIP phones, Yammer.com, and Google chat allow them to manage teams, collaborate with customers, and work on projects all while they are mobile. Every coffee shop (or beachfront lounge) in the world is their office. In the next chapter we go into depth and explore several guerrilla social media marketing weapons that will help you take your business virtual and mobile.

**STEPHEN JAGGER AND MICHAEL STEPHENSON,
GUERRILLA SOCIAL MEDIA PIONEERS**

Stephen Jagger and Michael Stephenson are fantastic examples of entrepreneurs that have pushed the limits on being virtual. About four years ago Steve and Mike's company, Ubertor.com, was based in an office in downtown Vancouver. Ubertor.com was then a real estate software company that operated like any technology company. It had expensive offices in Yaletown (the tech sector of downtown Vancouver), a pool table, a pinball machine, a theater, and about 25 workers.

Today, it operates completely virtually. Four years or so ago Steve and Mike decided to change the way they did business. Not only did they give up their swank offices, they also began the process of outsourcing and automating many of the day-to-day tasks in their business.

They began by moving some customer service duties to the Dominican Republic. The change from having their staff within arm's reach to having people they have never met required systems and procedures. This change helped cut costs but more importantly helped them continually systematize their internal processes.

After getting a taste of the cost savings of the Dominican Republic, Steve and Mike decided to see how they could tweak their business further. This drive to constantly improve brought them to Manila, Philippines. Their Manila team was put together originally as outsourced customer service and tech support. Ubertor was able to expand their roles to take over almost all of the day-to-day operations activities of the company.

While expanding their virtual team in Manila, Steve and Mike had repeated requests from other business owners to help them outsource their team. Initially Steve and Mike declined, explaining that they were not in the business of providing labor to other businesses. Then the recession hit in 2008, and they took a more serious look at starting an outsourcing business. OutsourcingThingsDone.com was born under the guidance of Steve and Mike and has grown into a fantastic business offering leased labor to small and medium businesses all over North America.

What tools do guerrilla entrepreneurs Stephen Jagger and Michael Stephenson use to manage their businesses?

- *Wikis.* Think employee manual, but instead of being paper based, Steve and Mike use online wikis to document all systems and procedures on an ongoing basis. Their wikis for all of their businesses have detailed information on the inner workings on their businesses, roles within them as well as all systems and procedures. This is what allows them to utilize staff all over the world and limit their exposure to the "hit by the bus factor" of employees leaving, quitting, etc. because all roles are documented.

- *Yammer*. Yammer.com is an online communication tool that Steve and Mike use as a tool for their behind-the-scenes communication. Yammer acts as their "watercooler." It's where all of the office chatter happens. When a new sale comes in, the team celebrates it together within Yammer. When a client asks a question to customer service that the customer service representative does not know, she can ask that question within Yammer. Ideally the answer to that question is within the wiki; if not, the answer is found through Yammer as well as documented within the wiki so that next time, that question can be answered by that customer service person.

- *VoIP*. Google Voice, Line2.com, and Skype are all great tools for phone management. Steve and Mike use combinations of all three to operate their business while keeping costs extremely low.

- *Google Docs*. Google Docs is where Steve and Mike store all spreadsheets and documents. This is how they can operate virtually from any computer at any time and still be able to manage their businesses. Google Docs is a fantastic way for a business with team members all over the world to share and collaborate quickly and easily.

Keep in mind for you as for Steve and Mike, it is not necessarily the specific tools but more the role that the tool provides. Companies and products/services will come and go, so focus on what these tools do, not the names. Think outside the box and work to systematize and document all procedures and roles within your business. Steve and Mike not only use the above tools but also Twitter, Facebook, Meetup.com, YouTube.com, Gmail.com, and many more to manage their operations.

6. FREE AND VARIABLE

It is important to use free digital giveaways that have real value and customer benefit. Then, of course, you need a variety of paid options to upgrade to. One-size-fits-all doesn't work anymore; people want very personalized options tailored to their particular taste and desires.

Lego.com effectively applies the concept of free and variable, and is profiting greatly from it. Using soft steps to gradually build consent from the customer is a key guerrilla strategy. Starting with free and highly interactive games, kids and adults alike quickly develop a loyalty and positive association to the Lego brand and the toys in the game. There's not one, two, or ten games; there are dozens with varying complexity and appeal.

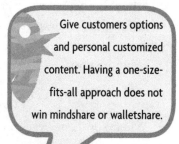

Give customers options and personal customized content. Having a one-size-fits-all approach does not win mindshare or walletshare.

Of course, the real winner is the free Lego DesignByMe downloadable software. This digital design software allows the user to virtually build Lego models using thousands of Lego pieces that are stored in its database. The user can rotate a 3D model in any direction, adding pieces, color, and functionality, and also calculating the exact cost of building and purchasing the model they have built.

Once they are happy with their unique design, which fits their personal budget, they then can even design a custom box cover and packaging. Lego will put all the pieces in the customer-designed box, complete with instructions to help the customer put together the model in real life. Lastly, they ship it to them directly from the factory.

The software has a social aspect as well, allowing members to add friends and also share and vote on designs. There's also several ways users can share their designs with friends and family who may want to purchase the custom Lego for them as a gift.

Free digital giveaways build trust and allow customers to experience your brand without risk. With trust you can garner consent to communicate and market to them. Variable customized options make it easier for customers to purchase and repurchase. In the case of Lego, there's always a new, exciting model to be purchased because the options are limitless.

7. REFERRAL AND REWARDS PROGRAM

Word-of-mouth is a very powerful way to market. In fact it's arguably the most powerful guerrilla marketing weapon that exists. Referral and rewards programs can help stimulate your word-of-mouth marketing. It is vital that you reward and promote those that promote you.

Paying It Forward First

When someone receives a genuine gift, compliment, or help from someone else, they often feel a sense of loyalty or even obligation. One of the best ways to generate goodwill within a business network is to promote those within the network before ever asking them for a lead or referral. In fact if a person or company significantly contributes to their network of business contacts or community, they often receive an ongoing stream of leads as time goes on.

From a social media and social networking perspective, promoting others could be done by

- blogging about someone and his business.
- posting positive feedback about her on Twitter, Facebook, or Google Buzz.
- doing a video testimonial for someone that you support.
- directly sending people links to leads or opportunities you find on the web.
- sharing value-added resources, studies, and information.

> Promote other people's dreams. It builds community, loyalty, and brand for you.

It is important to pay it forward, but it's also important to focus on the communities, niche markets, and clients that have the highest potential return on investment. Guerrillas invest heavily in their social equity with those that can influence their success. Your contribution must be focused and congruent with your business goals, brand, and positioning.

Reward Customers

Too many companies think their job is done once the client has been served or once their product has been received. That is actually when the work begins. Repeat business reduces marketing costs, and long-term customers tend to have greater loyalty and trust.

Rewards can come in many forms. Discounts on future purchases, the ability to test-drive a new product or software, or even one-on-one personal attention from staff and management can have a big impact on a customer's potential to repurchase. Sometimes a personalized thank-you e-mail or an update on Twitter to say how much you enjoyed working with the client can go a long way as well.

Formal member rewards programs that give points or discounts can also be effective. Remember, guerrillas always add value and are genuine. If you are going to have a rewards program, make it nonrestrictive, and easy to use, and make sure it has substantial benefits for your core target market. Frequent flyer programs with black-out periods, points programs that can only be used on the most expensive merchandise, or rewards that quickly expire are all examples of programs that miss the mark. Always make it easy for your ideal customer to do business with you.

Give Referral Fees or Gifts

Anyone who sends business your way should be rewarded. This reward can come in the form of merchandise, gift cards, VIP treatment, cash, or a big public thank-you. Some people and cultures expect a dinner as a thank you, others will be quite open to a cash reward. This is where knowing your customer and referral sources well is important.

Depending on the industry, some clients may not be able to accept gifts in some formats due to corporate governance rules. There are also FTC rules in the United States and equivalent laws in other countries that govern bloggers' activities online. If you are, in fact, giving gifts in lieu of payment for marketing or referrals, it is important that all parties involved openly disclose this relationship. The fines in the United States can exceed $20,000 per infraction.

Reward the Buzz

It's also important to reward those who positively promote your business. When a guerrilla asks a new customer "how did you find out about us" and the customer answers "you are everywhere," the guerrilla realizes that this has a lot to do with the buzz created by his network. Positive endorsements, casual referrals, and telling people how great your product is are all buzz-generating activities that people partake in.

If someone sends a lead to you, they should be rewarded, recognized, and made to feel appreciated regardless of the result. On a social network like Twitter or Google Buzz, it is as simple as making a list of the people who promote you or support you and making sure you do the same for them in a reasonable period of time.

Use Affiliate Software and Networks

Affiliate software allows a marketer to track who has referred business or leads. An affiliate marketer will set up an account using one of the many online affiliate marketing solutions available. She will then add products and payment options to the system. Once signed on as an affiliate, anyone who can publish a link embedded with a unique identifier code potentially becomes your marketing partner and generates income as a commission. When forming partnerships with other guerrillas, affiliate software can also help track the success and activity of each partner.

In the past website owners, forum participants, e-mail marketers, and bloggers made up the majority of affiliate marketers. Today anyone on Twitter, Facebook, Google Buzz, LinkedIn, or any of the thousands of other social networking sites can market your products or services for you.

8. LIKEABILITY

Social media is about being social. The guerrilla social media marketer is always working on being likable, therefore referable and credible. If people like you enough, they will find a reason to buy from you. Customer service can be defined in many ways, but boiled down to it's purest form, it's about making the customer feel totally wanted and appreci-

As a leader, make the journey look fun and share your joy. People will want to follow the path.

ated. Being likable is like having a giant blinking neon "Open for Business" sign above your head.

Likeable guerrilla social media marketers:

➤ *Only use their influence to positively build up people or create change.* Much of the noise on the internet is made up of self-important bloggers and social networkers who spend their time criticizing others. They also seem to always have a product, restaurant, politician, or unsuspecting community member that they are criticizing. It's very negative, and while we are marketing, it can dilute our message. Guerrilla marketers help customers reach personal goals, fulfill needs, and improve the lives and businesses of those around them. As a person's influence grows online and they see the real change and impact they can have on a community, they sometimes let it go to their head. With their Twitter cannon locked and loaded, they're ready to take down any business that doesn't treat them like royalty. Although this may at times be warranted, making a habit of it may not be great for most brands.

➤ *Always say thank you and recognize those who help them or promote their ideas.* Many people help us without any expectation of a returned favor. They may be fans, part of the community, or just genuinely think a product, service, or movement can help others. They will blog, tweet, and share their feelings. Guerrillas make sure that these people are thanked and truly feel appreciated. This also means when we are declared leaders by the community that we stay humble and publicly acknowledge that our position was earned through the help and support of those around us.

➤ *Respond quickly to public or private questions, comments, or concerns.* If you want to be liked, make others feel liked. When a question or comment comes in via Twitter, private message on Facebook, or is posted on your blog as a comment, make sure people are responded to quickly. One of the biggest criticisms of major brands online is the lack of responsiveness to questions, comments, or customer feedback. Many times brands don't have to be perfect; people will forgive companies and individuals for making mistakes. Today's highly wired culture is on 24 hours a day. Guerrillas know that immediate engagement is vital in becoming a likable company or individual.

→ *Don't argue or overreact to criticism, but respond and build bridges.* Many customers and online community members will criticize a company, its people, and its products, in many cases due to misinformation or misunderstanding. Guerrillas don't see this as an opportunity to publicly show someone up as wrong and defend their brand. Instead they see it as a way to further educate and inform these customers and strengthen their brand.

Many customers and community members may also feel uncomfortable if they are publicly engaged. Always give them the option to take it out of the public forum via telephone or e-mail.

→ *Are fun and funny.* What makes social media such an engaging set of tools is how fun they can be. The ability to freely converse and engage in personable, down-to-earth dialogue is what makes it so different from traditional marketing media. Aside from value-added interaction, entertainment and humor can build relationships and break down walls. Creativity and the element of surprise in our marketing is what will make us stand out.

It is important to note that no joke or marketing piece should defame, humiliate, or make fun of the brand. Your comments must be consistent with the brand and its positioning. The key tenant is have fun, but respect the brand.

→ *Are not pushy.* Respect boundaries, and take time to gain increasingly intimate levels of consent in marketing. Too many people connect on social networks, build a moderate level of rapport, and then aggressively go after an appointment or sale.

Remember that most social media interactions are text based or are not truly synchronous. This means it takes longer to gain rapport and trust. It is important that we respect each level of consent we get, respect boundaries, and move toward commercial interactions at a pace comfortable for our prospects.

Likeability and Credibility

Being likable plays a big role in being credible. The challenge for many marketers is they only have one speed or tonality. Why this is a challenge, is that credibility is contextual, meaning we all have unique credibility models. What some people would consider bold and innovative, others would consider loud and obscure. To identify what a market sees as credible requires a lot of in-depth interaction, feedback, and observation. Our credibility is vital as guerrilla marketers. Without it, our positioning, branding, and marketing is not believable. Many factors affect our credibility but here are a few to think about:

- ➤ *Observe with whom you are interacting and adjust accordingly*. Each nano-audience or subniche you are targeting will have subtle cultural, etiquette, and values differences. It's important that we observe these nuances and tweak our marketing message and approach for maximum credibility.
- ➤ *Keep promises*. Very few companies truly live the mission statement that is posted on the boardroom wall. Guerrillas know the power of keeping marketing promises and personal commitments. This is a massive advantage for anyone who does it right. Keeping promises builds trust, increases purchases, and builds credibility. Ultimately, credibility will drive loyalty, repeat purchases, and referrals.
- ➤ *Congruency*. Congruency is also very important in all things guerrillas do. Their level of professionalism and engagement

across all media and environments must be congruent. Once you have built rapport with a customer, he expects to have the same level of interaction and branding in all instances.

We went to our Facebook, Twitter, and Google Buzz following and here is what some of them said a likable social media marketer is:

- ➤ "I don't think you can look at being 'likeable' from a social media perspective. That's a personality set of traits." —Dr. Raul Pacheco (@hummingbird604)
- ➤ "Unique, clever, funny, kind, open-minded, knowledgeable, responsive, friendly, unpredictable . . . To name a few." —Kris Krug (@kk)
- ➤ "Being active in the social community and not using the different platforms for only 'business'." —Abraham Walker via Facebook (abrahamwalker.com)
- ➤ "Real conversation. What I love about my twitter feed is that I recognize the real people behind the handles. I've built relationships with these people, either by having conversations, retweeting, or just sending them a direct message. It's easy to be liked on a social networking website when you are recognized as a real person who will respond and be actively engaged in conversation." —Flowsion Shekar via Facebook (flowsion.net)
- ➤ "Nothing is more disappointing on social media [than] when you realize the person behind the tweets is not the person they say they are. Otherwise, likable Tweeps (people who use Twitter) are open, honest, transparent . . . what more could one ask for?" —Rick Rake (clickmediaworks.com)
- ➤ "I think inspiration is key. Has what they posted, blogged about, tweeted, etc. made you get up and do something?" —Thomas Morffew, Director at Ren Media via Google Buzz

9. TESTIMONIALS

Guerrillas seek out testimonials via blogger outreach and listen to what people say about their brand on Twitter, Facebook, Google Buzz, and dozens of other sites. They also do this by networking with other guerrillas to cross-endorse and promote.

A guerrilla testimonial strategy has to be in line with all of the attitudes and attributes that we have outlined in this book. What this means is that the testimonials are authentic and truly are a reflection of what you and your products and services represent to the community and your customer base.

A testimonial is in its purest form a written or spoken review of a product, service, company, or person. They are powerful because more and more people are searching out real customer feedback on products and services. As we have said before, they trust their friends and other people like themselves more than they trust the marketer.

Your testimonials are going to be very fragmented on the social web. It will be up to you to aggregate those comments, gain permission to use them, and then repurpose them for marketing.

Later in this book we discuss using guerrilla intelligence or social search tools to find people who are talking about you, your products, and your brand. These positive endorsements or feedback can happen on blogs, blog comments, Twitter, Facebook, YouTube, forums, or even on sites like Meetup.com.

It could be a simple one-line status update such as "I love my new Ford Flex, it is awesome in the snow." When a comment like this comes across a guerrilla's radar, they follow a specific process:

1. Thank the person for the positive comments publicly
2. Expand the endorsement to make it more specific by asking questions like:
   · What makes it so great in the snow?
   · Where have you been driving the vehicle?
   · What made you choose the vehicle?

3. After more rapport and dialogue, ask for permission and suggest attribution:
   - I'd like to post your comments on our community site. Would that be okay?
   - (If Yes) Could you send us a photo with you and the vehicle and the proper spelling of your name to give you credit?
4. After you have used the testimonial, thank the source and inform him of where it's posted and how it's being used. People will often share the link and information with friends and connections online.

It's important to not just wait for testimonials. Make it easy for people to promote you, and give positive feedback. This means having blog comments open and easy to post on your blog. It also means allowing people to post feedback on Facebook pages, profiles, groups, and any other site or social destination that you are part of.

Too many marketers moderate comments on their blog and social sites. This makes genuine people feel that the blog or forum is sanitized and inauthentic. Very few people want to post a testimonial or feedback if it has a chance of being edited or deleted. They also will mistrust the testimonials that have been approved.

Guerrillas are always ready to capture testimonials as well. This means carrying a video, photo, and audio capture device at all times. If a customer is in their store raving about service or how great a product is, politely ask them if they would put that in writing or allow you to take a quick 30-second video. The video or endorsement can be distributed on blogs, and in marketing materials, and also posted on YouTube, Facebook, and other major networks.

Believable testimonials use the person's first and last name and profession if appropriate. If the person is in video or audio, it's better to follow a slice of life or "guy on the street" type of production. Glossy testimonials shot in studios or staged environments are easy to spot and can often create mistrust instead of credibility. Guerrillas don't pay for endorsements or celebrity appearances; they use creativity, innovation, and the voice of the community to make their testimonials powerful.

10. REPUTATION

A reputation is a long-term bankable investment. Guerrillas base most of their decisions on preserving and building a reputation online and offline.

As much as 30 percent of the market capitalization of most of the top traded New York Stock Exchange-listed companies is based upon goodwill. After hard assets and earnings, these companies have billions of dollars in goodwill. In other words, based upon the company, its products, its patents, and its services, investors were willing to pay more than the value of the assets. They buy a dream or future promise of value based upon goodwill. A company's reputation tells people how often they keep the promises they make. The potential for a company to keep its promises affects its goodwill and its overall value in the marketplace.

Most guerrillas don't have billions of dollars in assets, patents, and inventory. Instead they have their creativity, innovation, and customer-centric values. What this means is that goodwill or reputation affects the guerrillas value in the marketplace even more than their large behemoth competitors or counterparts. Reputation is our number one asset as we build our brand.

A person can easily spend tens of thousands of dollars on a new website, blog, online advertising, search engine marketing, and contests. All of these things can buy traffic, clicks, and potentially sales. Unlike traffic, a reputation cannot be bought. It must be earned. A reputation in the social media and social networking space is built upon consistently producing great content, having meaningful conversations, and making great contributions to your network. This takes months or even years, and once earned, a strong online reputation is worth its virtual weight in gold. That reputation can also be lost so quickly that it leaves many brands terrified of even taking part in social media.

There are seven major areas of focus for guerrilla social media marketers to effectively manage, monitor, and build their reputation. They are

1. *Association.* The behavior, opinions, and business acumen of our friends and associates directly affect our reputation. Joining an organization's Facebook page, sharing someone's Tweet with your following, or linking to a blog can imply an endorsement by you and your brand. This also extends to staff that are representing you online. Hire the right people, and train them in the guerrilla attitudes, attributes, and strategies properly.

2. *Conflict management.* Getting into public debates, name-calling, or publishing angry posts or social status updates are all quick ways to erode one's reputation. If we are angry, highly critical, or publicly embarrass other people, this says a lot to our customers and prospects about how we will treat them or talk about them. Always take the high road and be a peacemaker.

3. *Brand monitoring.* People will make incorrect statements about brands online. They will also complain about products or services to their friends before going to the vendor. This unchecked negativity can grow like a weed in an untilled garden. Part of reputation management is using guerrilla intelligence tools to find this negativity or misinformation and then directly or indirectly addressing it proactively and in a timely manner.

4. *Customer experience.* Guerrillas' attention to details is what their reputation is built upon. This includes any and all points of contact and interaction with the customer involving the delivery of products and services. Everything from Twitter replies, website navigation, invoicing, and e-mail auto responders must be produced and executed in a way that creates an ideal customer experience at each touch point.

5. *Feedback.* Provide customers easy ways to give product and service feedback. Make it easy for them to express their challenges and angst, and make sure they feel heard and respected. By doing this we reduce the chance of negative feedback being posted and shared in places we cannot influence or moderate.

6. *Promises.* The more promises we make and keep, the better our reputation gets. Unmet marketing promises or even unmanaged customer expectations can really hurt our brand. When we continually make and keep promises, it builds trust with our customers and confidence within our own organization, and creates a strong communitywide reputation. Guerrillas make an inventory of promises and expectations, and systematically make sure they deliver on them.

7. *Truth.* Marketing is the truth made fascinating. Guerrilla social media marketing is about using all of the tools available to tell your fascinating brand story in a way that drives trust, consent, and profits. With that said, guerrillas tell the truth, and they tell the whole truth. With social media networks and platforms, the millions of people that inhabit them quickly detect lies or half-truths. Misinformation or false pretenses can be profitable in the short term, but over the long term not telling the truth will destroy your trust, credibility, and ultimately your fragile reputation.

You now have a strong foundation and understanding of the core attitudes, attributes, and characteristics of a successful guerrilla social media marketer. Technology, trends, and our community will evolve, but these principles are timeless and will serve you today and five years from today as a guerrilla social media marketer.

In the next few chapters we help you select your marketing weapons and then build your social media launch plan.

CHAPTER 4

THE GUERRILLA
SOCIAL MEDIA
ARSENAL

Now that you have a foundation and an understanding of the path and ethos of guerrilla social media marketing, we will help you choose and arm yourself with the most effective guerrilla social media marketing weapons.

As with any profession, guerrillas need tools to perform their trade. In this case you must select and master a set of guerrilla social media weapons that will help you achieve your business goals. The following pages outline the core hardware, software, and social media weapons that guerrilla social media marketers need to use effectively.

We have listed over 100 weapons and tools. Most guerrillas will only use 10 or 15 of them in their ongoing marketing campaigns. This list could feel overwhelming for some. With that said, it's important to be aware of all of the tools and, over time, experiment with individual weapons and combinations of weapons to find what works best for you, your company, and your customers. It gives you freedom and flexibility. It gives you options and power.

100+ GUERRILLA SOCIAL MEDIA WEAPONS AND TOOLS

Hardware Tools

The guerrilla social media marketer needs hardware. In order to outsmart, outwork, and outconnect the competition, guerrillas need hardware that allows them to create and distribute content anywhere and at anytime. Here are some of the key tools needed:

> Fresh valuable content beats perfect outdated content every time. Use tools that help you publish easy and fast.

1. Smartphone with a Data Plan

Social media is going more mobile by the minute. Having a good smartphone is important. iPhones, Blackberries, Google Phones, some Nokia handsets, and an increasing number of other phones fall into this category. Make sure before investing in this tool that it supports the social network applications and publishing platforms that you will be using. You'll be surprised how often they don't. Smartphones free you from any particular location and allow you to be a completely mobile social media publisher and connector.

2. Notebook Computer

A powerful and portable notebook computer is vital. It will allow you to process video files, edit images, record podcasts, and communicate with the world. A desktop computer isn't suitable unless you expect to do all of your social media marketing from one place. Guerrillas need horsepower to move fast, process quickly, and publish fast. You want to be able to process files, video, and downloads, and communicate with others at the same time. Make sure you don't trade too much power for looks, trendiness, or an overly compact computer.

3. Video Camera

Get a video camera that is user friendly and highly compatible with multiple computer operating systems. Most videos produced by guerrillas are more personal than they are professional, and that is a key to their effectiveness. Your major concern should be ease of use and distribution. In other words, buy a video camera that is easy to record with in formats that are easy to import, edit, and upload to sites like YouTube. If you can't shoot, edit, and upload a ten-minute clip in less than an hour, you have the wrong video camera. It's that simple.

4. Digital Camera

Guerrillas are great storytellers. Cpturing a story at an event or function with pictures is a powerful guerrilla tactic. Taking photos of yourself with industry leaders and celebrities or snapping a shot of a happy customer is a great way to tell a story.

5. Good Microphone

Invest in a high-quality but easy-to-use microphone. This will be used to record seminars, client interviews, experts, testimonials, podcasts, and a myriad of other media. It's easy to create a professional-sounding recording with a good mic.

6. Boingo Wifi Membership

Without connectivity all of the great hardware in the world will not help you. For a monthly membership fee, you can have access to 125,000+ wireless internet locations globally, including, Starbucks, MacDonald's, and most major airports and hotels. This combined with your notebook computer gives you 125,000-plus guerrilla outposts from which to do business. Wireless access is easy to take for granted, but don't fall into that trap.

7. Webcam

Video chat, live streaming, and many webinar platforms require you to have a webcam. This could be built into your computer or can be purchased as a separate USB device. Video is important because as guerrillas know, rapport is a key element in gaining permission to market and sell to people. If used effectively, video can be a big rapport builder because of its personal aspect.

Software Tools

The guerrilla needs the right software to create content, gather intelligence, and connect with the world.

8. Graphic and Photo Editing Software

Whether you're using a Mac or a PC, there are dozens of great photo editing and graphics programs available that are easy to use. You may need it to crop an avatar or brighten a photo from an event. With a little training or trial and error, you can learn to create attractive digital marketing pieces using this software. You're not trying to become a graphic designer; you're just making sure you are as self-sufficient as a guerrilla needs to be.

9. Audio Editing Software

There are easy-to-use audio editing and conversion software suites in the marketplace. The most common ones today are Garage Band for

Mac and Audacity for the PC. We suggest these because they are the easiest to use and require very little training. The shorter the learning curve, the quicker you can start producing great podcasts and audio sound bites.

10. Video Editing Software

Both Macs and PCs come with some great video editing software already on them. iMovie for Mac or Windows Movie Maker for the PC should serve the needs of most people and are very simple to use. If you want to begin producing more high-end productions or adding complex transitions or green-screened productions, then Final Cut Pro would be a good software choice. Final Cut takes longer to master but there are literally thousands of free video tutorials on YouTube on using all of these video editing software suites. It's best to watch some before you make your purchase so you know what you're getting into.

11. Contact/Customer Relationship Management Software

Guerrillas know that their customer list is one of their most important assets, and they use a system to track and organize their sales and marketing activities. Keeping track of contacts and customers using contact management or CRM (Customer Relationship Management) software is important and easier than you may imagine. Microsoft, SalesForce.com, Oracle, and hundreds of other companies provide these tools. Pick one that you find intuitive and easy to use, then use it to drive your sales process with the leads and contacts you create in the social media space. Tracking makes follow-up easy.

12. Browser with Social and Google Plug-Ins

Many of the social media weapons we discuss in this chapter are accessed via a web browser. By using a browser that is compatible with toolbars and plug-ins from social media and social networking sites, guerrillas are able to automate or speed up a lot of activities.

Firefox and Internet Explorer are the most plug-in-friendly browsers. Some of the plug-ins and toolbars you should install are:

- ➤ The Google Toolbar
- ➤ LinkedIn Companion for Firefox
- ➤ LinkedIn Toolbar for Outlook
- ➤ StumbleUpon Toolbar
- ➤ Share on Facebook Widget
- ➤ Digg Toolbar
- ➤ Addthis browser plug-in

Social Networking

Social networks are where you forge relationships, recruit other guerrillas, gather intelligence, and generate qualified business leads and contacts. Some of the social networks have been broken down into separate individual weapons because each has a unique application and purpose in your arsenal. Not everyone will use every aspect or function of every social network. What you do use depends on your goals, target market, launch plan, and social media calendar. The major tools and networks are:

13. Facebook Profile

Facebook is approaching over 400 million registered users globally, more than the entire population of the United States. Within its virtual walls reside many lucrative demographics; indeed, you can think of Facebook as one of the richest "nations" on the planet. In order to engage, attract, and develop contacts, you need to have a Facebook profile. Think of it as the front page of your very personal website. It's not a landing page; it's an engagement page. Include photos, videos, complete personal and business information, and anything else that will help you establish trust and credibility. You're looking for permission to connect with people, and you need to have a complete and professional profile to achieve this.

14. Facebook Pages

Facebook Pages are very similar in functionality to Facebook Profiles. They're basically profiles, but for businesses, brands, or even products. It's a mistake to make a Profile for anything other than an individual human being; Facebook will delete it. Use Pages instead. You can install custom applications that drive marketing and even capture leads, data, and demographic information. Multiple administrators within a company or community can be set up to manage the page, which can reduce its impact on the time and resources of any one individual. The big advantage of Pages over Facebook Groups is the ability to communicate to your fans via updates that will appear on their homepages when they log into Facebook. (Use discretion when broadcasting. People can disconnect from you forever or mute you with one click.)

15. Facebook Groups

Guerrillas use Facebook Groups for creating communities or gathering people of similar interests and values or who share the same goals. Groups are more private than Pages and can be set up as invite-only or can be opened up to the world. This depends on their intended purpose. Unlike Pages, group members know the administrator's identity. Conversations, content, and actions within the group can impact your personal brand. Unlike Pages, group admins communicate via direct message vs. status updates. This is limited to 5,000 group members per broadcast. If managed well from a leadership perspective, being an admin for a group can increase engagement and deepen relationships with the community.

16. Facebook Events

A page, group, or individual can organize Facebook Events. The Facebook Events tool is free and very easy to use; with it you can organize and invite people to an event. When people RSVP, their network will often be notified; this creates the potential for news about your event to go viral and extend to people you don't know or directly influence. People can upload images, video, and links, and add comments to the event page if you allow them to. Attendees can also invite their list of friends on Facebook, once again adding a powerful viral or leveraged element to promoting an event.

17. Facebook Applications

Facebook has a function that allows individuals and pages to install extra applications. These applications add extra functionality and networking ability to a basic Facebook Profile. Customized applications can cost anywhere from a few hundred to several thousand dollars to build but can be very valuable to a guerrilla marketer. Some types of applications include:

- ➤ Contest and refer-a-friend apps
- ➤ Games that are branded and capture leads
- ➤ Document, video, and image-sharing apps
- ➤ Coupon marketing apps
- ➤ E-commerce apps that are embedded within Facebook
- ➤ Geo/location-based apps

18. LinkedIn Profile

LinkedIn is a destination for professionals to meet and share trusted connections. It is one of the oldest and most respected social networking sites in the world. Many senior executives, future employers, and potential fusion partners will check you out on LinkedIn before doing business with you. Have a complete profile with your entire relevant job or entrepreneurial history. Include a professional photograph and also make sure you complete your contact information. Remember, guerrillas are social and are open to connecting and growing their networks; go into your privacy settings and make sure that people are able to view your profile publicly. Be aware of the differences in professionalism between LinkedIn and Facebook.

19. LinkedIn SlideShare

This application allows you to share your most recent PowerPoint presentations and documents publicly on LinkedIn. Being seen as an authority, expert, or author in a specific area or discipline can help establish trust and credibility. SlideShare allows you to showcase this right on your LinkedIn profile.

20. LinkedIn Google Presentations

Similar to LinkedIn's app SlideShare, Google's app allows you to share presentations you've created using its hosted presentation application. Because of the features and options within Docs to combine and integrate many types of files, media, and tools, it can add a whole new level of engagement and connection opportunities to your LinkedIn profile. One fantastic feature is your ability to embed a YouTube video into a presentation; this feature provides you with a back-door opportunity to post marketing videos right on your LinkedIn profile.

21. LinkedIn Twitter

LinkedIn and Twitter can easily be integrated by activating your Twitter account within your LinkedIn profile. By doing this, you can allow Twitter to publish links, updates, and information as LinkedIn status updates. The more often you update your status with relevant business information, the more likely your contacts are to notice you. One note of caution: People use LinkedIn differently than Twitter; LinkedIn is a business-only professional network. If you update Twitter a lot, especially about nonbusiness topics, you may not want to tether the two accounts. Too many updates could cause other professionals to delete you as a contact because you are too noisy.

22. LinkedIn Blog Import

Both the Blog Link and WordPress applications allow you to automatically update your LinkedIn Profile with information and links to your most recent blog entries. It's a way to ensure that your profile is dynamic and always current. In addition, any of your connections that use these tools will also see your recent blog entries as a feed on their homepage when they visit LinkedIn.

23. LinkedIn Groups

LinkedIn Groups allows you to create groups based on an almost unlimited number of topics. You can create your own group and invite your network and contacts to join. As a guerrilla, you can also join other communities that cater to your target market to expand your network and prospect base. This is also a great way to identify and partner with other guerrillas who have a large sphere of influence within your target markets. Group access can vary from open and public to completely private, depending upon how you want to use them.

24. LinkedIn Answers

LinkedIn Answers has many possible uses. With Answers you can search for topics that relate to your area of expertise; you will then find questions that you can ask. You will even be prompted to provide additional links to content, which could (if relevant) drive traffic to your blog or an outside site. Members vote on the answers, and you can begin to develop a ranking as an expert on a topic area within LinkedIn. People with challenges that fall into your potential target market or niches are also easy to identify within Answers, based upon the questions they are answering. To gather intelligence a guerrilla can also post questions that will help them find solutions and identify potential fusion partners.

25. LinkedIn Events

Once you have established a network of trusted contacts, you can begin to use LinkedIn Events. LinkedIn Events are a great way to take your online contacts offline or to fill an online webinar. When someone RSVPs, in many cases their network is notified, providing opportunities for the event marketing to go viral. You can also search within LinkedIn Events via topic and geography to find conferences and events that would have a high concentration of prospective clients and alliances in attendance. LinkedIn will also let others that are not part of your network know about your event if it is a subject of interest to them.

26. Orkut

Orkut is not a well-known network in North America. But, if you are an international marketer and networker and want to connect with people in Brazil and India, Orkut is a great vehicle for doing so. The majority of users are between 18 and 30 years old and over 70 percent are from India and Brazil. This is a particularly desirable demographic to those selling and marketing to consumers.

27. Hi5

Available in over 25 languages, this network has a high concentration of users outside of North America. Much like Orkut, Hi5 is a dominant network in some regions that those who are global marketers may want to reach. Some of the countries where Hi5 is very popular are: Mexico, Honduras, Nicaragua, Guatemala, Costa Rica, Colombia, Ecuador, Peru, Romania, Portugal, Thailand, and Mongolia. Hi5 has a mobile component, and many members accesses it via mobile devices. This network is very popular with the under-30 demographic. It's important to note that the average age of an adult in these countries is from the mid- to late-20s, and they represent a very specific market.

28. Xing

This network is a direct competitor for LinkedIn in Europe; in Germany it is one of the dominant players. Xing has close to 4 million members and is available in 16 languages. In many regions there are

Xing member events that are actively promoted and officially supported by Xing. This provides a unique blend of online and offline networking that few social networks today provide. If you are in the business-to-business marketing space and Europe is a market for you, Xing is a must-join.

29. Ecademy

A highly social network, it doesn't boast millions of members, but from our experience, the members on this site are very social and are entrepreneurial by nature. Most members are self-employed, over the age of 40, and reside in Europe. The biggest demographic representation is in the UK. With a little proactivity you can establish new business contacts here. The site provides a number of options for publishing and distributing your social media content, including blog entries, video, and photos. In order to fully benefit from this tool, you need to invest in a paid membership. If your target clients or fusion partners are entrepreneurs in Europe, the investment may be worth it.

30. Brazencareerist.com

Guerrillas should always be looking for new talent and innovative thinkers. Brazen Careerist started as a Generation Y (those born after 1980) blogging network and has morphed into a social network complete with a full profile and resume tab for each member. It also provides a thought stream, a series of recent comments, and personal updates on the profile. It is a great site to get direct feedback and information from Generation Y and to meet this tribe of online entrepreneurs and influencers.

White-Labeled Networks

Although there are options within Facebook, LinkedIn, and almost every other social network to create and host groups or communities, at times we will need more control and ownership of the community we create. White-labeled networks, social network platforms that you host and brand as your own, can serve this purpose. They require a financial investment in order to have your network customized by a designer, but it is well worth it over the long term.

31. Ning.com

Ning is one of the most cost-efficient and easy-to-deploy networks. Millions of networks and communities use the Ning community platform. You can register and have your community hosted as a subdomain (yourname.ning.com) or for a few more dollars a month at your own domain (yourname.com). By paying the few extra dollars a month, you can choose which (if any) ads appear and have total control over the branding, look, feel, and functionality of the site. As the owner and founder, you can also distribute messages directly to the entire base. The community manager can also determine what videos, blogs, pictures, and links are displayed on the most popular sections of the network.

32. BuddyPress

This social network tool is actually comprised of several WordPress plug-ins that together take a normal WordPress blog and add social network functionality to it. This includes member profiles, forums, blogs, activity streams, private messages, and the ability to friend someone or add a connection. As each function is driven by separate plug-ins, you can have some or all of the functionality integrated into your blog. BuddyPress literally can take a standard WordPress blog and fully transition it into a community hub or portal.

33. Enterprise-Level White-Label Networks

If you're looking to build very large corporate communities or build social networks for global brands and organizations, an enterprise-level software solution may be needed. Some of the top-rated vendors and solutions you may want to check into are: Jive Software, Pluck, Awareness, and Acquia Drupal, and there are dozens more. Forrester Research and Gartner Research both publish studies and profiles several times per year on these software solutions. Guerrillas think long term when they make marketing investments; make sure the software company you choose has great functionality, a strategic vision, and financial stability. Invest in some of these studies and do research on your vendors to protect your investment and resources.

Nano-Blogging Weapons

The nano-blogging weapons are some of the most viral and easy to use in the guerrilla's arsenal. Guerrillas use nano-blogging tools for broadcasting, research, listening, conversations, and identifying prospective clients. These are simple-to-use, multipurpose, high-concentration marketing tools. They are called nano-blogging tools because of their small size (most are only 140 characters per update) and the ease with which they can move around our very large planet.

34. Twitter

At the time of writing, Twitter is one of the most talked about and utilized guerrilla social media marketing weapons. A favorite of Fortune 500 marketing teams and individual entrepreneurs, Twitter has set the tone for how status updates and nano-blogging are done. With a series or stream of updates limited to 140 characters each, guerrillas get to do what they're great at: tell a story. People often ask, "Who cares what you're doing? Why do people broadcast their thoughts 140 characters at a time?" But

Nothing happens until someone tweets something.

we know that people love stories, and at a 140 characters at a time you can tell the world about your brand, your passions, your community, what you love, and what you stand for. You can also use it to simply say "Hey I'm listening to you and I'm accessible." Something that customers love.

Twitter allows people to learn more about you, and to deepen relationships with your brand in easily digestible bites.

35. Complete Twitter Profile

Many people start following people and having conversations before they have a complete profile set up. In order to maximize engagement and really build credibility, make sure you take time to complete your profile. A complete profile has:

- A link to your website or blog so that people can learn more about you.
- The 160-character bio completed in your profile.
- A customized background that is complete with your picture, logo, corporate colors, and contact details (all on a single graphic).
- At least 20 valuable Tweets (updates) on your profile before you begin connecting with others.

36. Public Twitter Lists

Within Twitter you will need to use the lists function to begin to organize those people you want to follow and assign them to a list. Once you are following the updates of 100 people or more, you will need to follow their updates by breaking them into smaller manageable lists based upon topic, industry, and importance to you. Public lists of people on Twitter provide you an opportunity to

- Let people know why you think they are important.
- Help others find great people on Twitter, which builds community and positions you as a connector.

37. Private Twitter Lists

Private lists serve a different purpose. They are part of your guerrilla intelligence toolkit. Use them to aggregate customers, competitors, valuable information sources, and people with whom you want to cement relationships. Keep these lists private so that competitors don't know your key contacts or clients, and so that your clients aren't aware of just how closely you're watching and monitoring them.

38. Status Updates

In addition to Twitter, most social networking and member-based sites give you the ability post a status update of 140 characters or fewer. You can tell your network or maybe the whole world what you're doing, or share a valuable or entertaining link or thought with them. With Facebook, LinkedIn, Ning, Google, and many of the smaller sites with social functionality, this option is open to you. Guerrillas make sure they keep fresh and valuable updates on all of their major networks because they know the importance of frequency in gaining mindshare and, in turn, walletshare.

39. Friendfeed

A dynamic social media aggregation tool, Friendfeed allows you to pull in all of your blogging, status updates, photo sharing, video sharing, comments, and bookmarks into one RSS-driven stream. You can then connect with people on the system just like you would in Twitter by following their updates. You can also post updates directly from Friendfeed and update Twitter, Facebook, and almost any web-based application that integrates with an RSS feed. It really is an integrated tool allowing you to listen, gather intelligence, post updates, comment on updates, and make new connections.

40. URL shorteners

When you have as few as 140 characters to post status updates, you don't want to waste the space with long website urls and page links.

Url shortners will take a long domain such as: gmarketing.com/tips /read/3458/tip.html and create a link to the same page that looks something like this: http://ow.ly/1p5xv.

Services like Bit.ly and Ow.ly both also have in-depth statistical data available. They tell you the time and date of the clicks you get on the links you publish. This data also includes the number of clicks and the geographic region they come from. As a marketer, this allows you to test which status updates are most effective. It also tells you what time of day and what regions give you the best click-through rates.

Third-Party Social Networking Applications

Guerrillas are focused and organized. Being on several social networks and having several hundred or even several thousand contacts can amount to a lot of noise and distraction. By having a system and process for organizing your contacts and conversations, you can execute your marketing efficiently.

41. Tweetdeck

This application allows you to view updates from Twitter, Facebook, LinkedIn, and MySpace all in one dashboard. It supports multiple Twitter accounts as well. You can also view, record, and share video within this application. Within the desktop application you can create groups of contacts or use the Twitter List function to aggregate your contact base. This is important because it allows you to listen to and nano-cast to nano-tribes within your target markets.

42. HootSuite

HootSuite started off with functionality similar to TweetDeck's but has some major differences. First, the application is web-based, so there's no need to store data. Anyone with an up-to-date web browser can easily use it. HootSuite is fully integrated with Twitter lists. You can view updates on Facebook, Facebook Pages, Multiple Twitter Accounts, LinkedIn, and WordPress blogs, and post comments and nano-casts to specific segments and groups. It also allows you to manage multiple Twitter accounts and Facebook pages. Designed with the business user in mind, this tool is guerrilla approved. HootSuite also has in-depth analytical reporting on click-through rates for links, including the time of day and geographic regions that produced the click-throughs.

43. SocialToo

This tool automates the following and following-back of other Twitter users. You can program it to follow anyone who mentions a certain keyword term in his tweets. These accounts are added to a list that you can either automatically approve or manually review and approve one by one. It allows you to grow your Twitter following with very little effort in a very short period of time. Use this tool with caution; following too many people and automating too many Twitter updates and processes will have you labeled as a spammer by the community.

44. Seesmic

This is another Twitter application that is similar to HootSuite and TweetDeck. Historically it was more focused, in the sense that it only managed Twitter, Twitter Search, and Twitter lists. Its recent purchase of and merger with Ping.fm now allows Seesmic to update more than 50 social networks at once. Seesmic comes in a desktop and web-based format.

45. Ping.fm

Guerrillas need to be everywhere at once. Even if we're niche-focused marketers we still have a lot of territory to cover. Ping.fm is a web-based application that allows you to connect and broadcast to more than 50 social networks from one console. It is very platform-agnostic, so you don't even need a computer or a smartphone to use it. From any text messaging-enabled phone you can send a message to Ping.fm, and it will send it out to all of the networks you are connected to. A word of caution: if you're connected to the same people on several networks, identical status updates that are impersonal could lead people to see you as insincere or disengaged.

Photo Sharing

Photo sharing or web albums are fantastic guerrilla tools. They allow you to share images of your brand and events, and can also be used for contests and promotions. You can re-use and redistribute your images onto other platforms such as blogs, Facebook, or some mobile applications. Some people use photo-sharing sites as a visual life stream, updating their network with their personal story and their brand story one photo at a time. After viewing a few hundred photos of your events and activities, many people will feel they know you because they have experienced your life and your brand through the lens of your camera. Many times other people will also upload and add photos of you, your products, and your business, adding to your online brand with user-generated content.

46. Flickr

Flickr is the dominant photo-sharing site on the web. It allows you to post your photos for the entire world to see. You can decide what type of copyright and level of sharing (from very public to very private) that you want to have for each picture you upload. Flickr has a large, vibrant community of people and interest-based groups where you can add connections, share and showcase photos, and find nano-tribes of people interested in specific topics, products, and movements. In order to display and access more than 200 photos, you must upgrade to a Pro account. The fee is less than $3 per month. Flickr also has the highest traffic of all photo-sharing sites, and therefore the greatest potential to gain you exposure. Flickr has a video-sharing utility as well. Additionally, it is extremely professional looking, in contrast to some other photo-sharing sites.

47. Picasa

A photo-sharing site, Picasa is owned by Google and has a less visually appealing user interface than Flickr. It is easy to learn in comparison to Flickr, but is not that well integrated with third-party sites and applications. If you want to engage professional photographers and the tech-savvy crowd, you may not find them on Picasa. If your target market is the consumer market and less technologically sophisticated people, this may be the right site for your photos.

Document Sharing

A lot of the content that you will share, market, and promote will come in the form of documents. These documents can be studies, short e-books, presentations, technical information, and marketing materials. You can of post these documents on your own web server and market them directly off your site. For greater exposure you can upload them and submit them to document-sharing websites. These websites have social networking components to them and are often well liked by Google. By using document-sharing sites guerrillas can identify new markets, prospects, and alliances and expand their reach.

48. SlideShare

If you do presentations and use tools like PowerPoint or Keynote, SlideShare can help you showcase your knowledge, expertise, service, and product presentations. SlideShare has done for documents what YouTube has done for video. You can upload presentations with a variety of options for sharing. There's also an option to choose whether the presentation can be downloaded or only viewed on the page. Presentations can also be made private and only shared via a private link with specific people. SlideShare helps you create high visibility for your presentations and also allows others to embed the document in their site or blog, giving you even greater reach. It is possible to embed audio and even Youtube videos into the presentations, making them a true multimedia experience.

49. Scribd

When Chris Anderson released his book *Free: The Future of a Radical Price* (Hyperion, 2009), he first posted the entire book on Scribd for free. Over 170,000 people viewed the book online and shared it with others during the book launch. Within days the book made the *New York Times* bestseller list. Scribd is a great way to share free reports, white papers, books, and anything else that you want to distribute. You can also embed Scribd document HTML code into online press releases and websites. Many of the book views were actually as a result of bloggers embedding it in their sites.

Audio and Video

Audio and video recordings are powerful media that can add an additional element of rapport and engagement that text and web chat cannot. Video and audio can spark emotion, grab attention, or just plain annoy people, depending on how you use them. You can literally be the host of your own interest radio show or newscast with these easy-to-use, highly distributable mediums.

50. Podcasts

A podcast is more than an MP3 file. It is in essence a series of audio episodes on a certain topic. These episodes are accessible via a web browser and often can be played right on the website that hosts them. What makes a podcast powerful is that people can also subscribe to and download the MP3 (audio files) to their computer or a mobile device like an MP3 player or smartphone. Even when someone is not online, she can take you and your show anywhere. Many executives listen to their favorite business podcasts when they are at the gym, driving their car, or on a plane. This highly distributable file is often shared with their contacts, friends, and staff if they find the content valuable. The cost of producing a podcast can be pennies. Podcasts can help attract new business leads, and nurture and develop existing clients. If they're popular enough, you can even sell advertising on them.

Video Sharing

Video-sharing sites give you the ability to easily distribute video content that you have created. You can post corporate videos and marketing pieces, but traditional marketing videos don't tend to work well over the long term on video-sharing sites. In most cases the most successful video-marketing formats for guerrillas are video series that are produced in an almost amateur fashion. Episodic programs can build strong and loyal subscriber bases if they're produced effectively and consistently.

51. YouTube

Guerrillas market where their customers are. Because YouTube has several hundred million video views per day, your customers are most likely there. You can record a video and upload the digital file to the site or use your webcam to allow it to directly capture your message on its servers.

52. Viddler

Another popular video site has a couple of important differences with YouTube. With a standard YouTube account, your videos cannot be longer than ten minutes, which is not the case with Viddler.

Viddler is great for hosting full training videos, tutorials, and your own internet TV shows that require longer, higher resolution. In addition, you are able to brand your video player with your own corporate colors and logo.

53. Niche and specialty networks

There are many niche video-sharing networks on the web. With some of them it is easier to find and target certain types of prospects and markets than it is on one of the large sites. Also, when you're targeting international markets you will need to look at producing video in that language and uploading it to local language sites. Here are some examples of niche and/or non-English video sites:

- *Vimeo*: Noncommercial arts and original content site.
- *FameCast*: Music-only site for emerging artists.
- *Blip.tv*: Used primarily for web video shows, easy to syndicate and integrates well with major blogging platforms.
- *Facebook Video*: Allows you to share video with your friends only or to make video available in public search.
- *Vbox7.com*: The largest video-sharing site in Bulgaria.
- *Nico Nico Douga*: Nicovideo.jp is a popular video-sharing site in Japan.
- *Tudou*: A Chinese video-sharing site serving Greater China. According to its site it serves more video than YouTube.

54. Video Contest Software

There are dozens of video-driven contest sites available on the internet. We were contacted directly by Strutta, a company that is successfully using user-generated video to increase sales, build lists, and engage existing customers for their clients.

Contests with UGC (user-generated content) have a viral potential that puts the marketing into the hands of contestants. A video or photo contest that is decided by a popular vote encourages contestants to get out and spread the word, driving traffic to your campaign.

Strutta makes this easy by including "share" tools with every entry and integration with popular networks like Facebook and Twitter. Each entry has its own individual link, making it easy for contestants to reach their existing networks or share entries directly to friends via e-mail.

With the right mix of relevant promotion, exciting prizes, and active marketing execution, a contest can yield excellent results ranging from visibility and data collection to sales. To keep contests fair, Strutta monitors and tracks fraudulent voting activity, and offers moderation options and the ability to select contest winners with a panel of judges, offering brands that are new to the social media space the protection they often insist upon. Custom survey question options let marketers collect relevant data during the contest registration process, and the resulting info can be downloaded as a spreadsheet.

HOW TWO COMPANIES USED STRUTTA AS A GUERRILLA SOCIAL MEDIA MARKETING WEAPON

CRATE & BARREL

In early 2010, Crate & Barrel launched a wedding giveaway contest with Strutta (ultimateweddingcontest.com/). Couples were asked to submit a photo of themselves, answer three short essay questions, and complete a Crate & Barrel gift registry. Their pending nuptials had to exceed 50 line items and $2,000 worth of products. The prize was a $100,000 wedding, planned by celebrity wedding planner Jo Gartin.

By offering a great prize as incentive and directly targeting the wedding vertical, Crate & Barrel received close to 9,000 entries, and the majority of those entries represented new gift registries at Crateandbarrel.com. Even without knowing the exact conversion figures on gift registries, it's easy to see how this campaign generated plenty of awareness and loads of great content, but also saw a significant return in terms of new customers and sales.

ADORAMA

Adorama, a popular U.S.-based photography retailer, held an iPhone photo contest with Strutta, and accepted entries via mobile upload. The grand prize was a $1,000 gift card from Adorama, and several hundred secondary prizes were given as well. The contest generated over 12,000 entries, and contestants were asked a series of questions about the iPhone apps they used to edit their entry.

In the end, the contest was a huge success for Adorama in terms of community engagement, generating new business, and collecting valuable data about the applications its customers use regularly.

Real-Time Social Media

Some of the most engaging social media are real-time social media. This is the future of social media marketing, but it's here now in many forms. Live video broadcasting with audience interaction, real-time blog updates, and video chat rooms are all tools that you can use to connect directly with your existing and prospective clients.

There are thousands of real-time tools being developed. The best ones allow for bi-directional communications. That is, they are tools that help you have real-time conversations with people. We have listed a few that we feel are well above the crowd.

55. Ustream

This site allows you to easily broadcast live video feeds to the web. If you have a webcam and a microphone, it can take less than ten minutes to set up your account and begin broadcasting. Viewers can communicate with you and the rest of the audience via the chat console. Ustream can also integrate with Twitter. It has several slide- and presentation-sharing plug-ins that can turn it into an online seminar tool. Ustream is capable of working with high-end digital video cameras as well, but that feature is known to be challenging to set up. Definitely do a dry run well before any live broadcast to test your settings.

56. Justin.tv

This service is very similar to Ustream. Many users claim that Justin.tv has a higher quality video stream and better technical support. Also, independent reviews show the service to be more stable. It takes a lot of effort to build an audience that will watch any video show, so making sure the show is stable and stays online is critical.

57. Skype

This tool does a number of things for a guerrilla. It allows you to video chat for free with anyone else who has a Skype account (and a good internet connection). Skype also allows you to make free, or almost free, calls to anyone on the planet. In addition, you can use it to record podcast interviews and important client calls (with their permission of course). Additional built-in features are chat, group chat, conference calling, and screen sharing for client presentations, sales pitches, and training.

58. Coveritlive

It is the leading live-blogging and live-event tool and can be embedded into almost any blog or web page. Most major tech product launches and conferences include a live-blogging component to the event. It allows those attending to have a central place to communicate and comment about the event, and it also allows you to expand the reach of the event onto the internet to those who could not attend. Coveritlive also integrates with Twitter, video-streaming services, and photo posting. In addition, it can be organized into a panel, allowing several experts or organizers to contribute at once. The result is a real-time blog entry that grows throughout the event and can be replayed as an archived event indefinitely. You can blog from a web-connected computer or several types of smartphones and mobile devices.

59. TinyChat

It is a very simple and easy-to-use video conferencing tool that hosts up to nine people for a conference or to chat for free. It has a screen-sharing utility and audio and text chat as well. With a little help from a web developer, you can host one of these chatrooms on your own site as well. With the click of a button you can announce the event or meeting to your Twitter following and Facebook connections, and bring them into the conversation.

60. Webcasts and Web Conferencing

GoToMeeting, Webex, and DimDim are all great web conferencing tools. Webinars are fantastic tools to engage and educate your prospects and client base. GoToMeeting and WebEx are both very scalable and can handle very large audiences. DimDim on the other hand, has a free service for conferencing and webinars for groups of fewer than 20 people.

61. Screencasting

This technology allows you to capture whatever you are displaying on your computer screen. Screencasting allows you to create videos of software demonstrations, PowerPoint, or keynote presentations, and even integrate other videos and effects into it. The software ranges from free basic online capture tools to high-end professional quality software.

Instead of listing the features and benefits of your products or services on a static website page, you can create highly engaging and educational videos. They can be used for training, building infotainment products, or presenting a marketing idea, product, or proposal. Just like any other video, screencasts can be widely distributed and shared by bloggers and through communities like YouTube.

Website and Blog Tools

Websites and blogs are a guerrilla's core branding and marketing hub. They are your home base. In order to truly turn your website or blog into a real guerrilla marketing weapon you will need to integrate several of the weapons and plug-ins discussed in this section. While social networking sites are great guerrilla outposts where you can make new connections, your blog or website is your guerrilla headquarters. This is where you will establish credibility for your brand, educate prospects and customers, and aggregate all of your social media content.

62. Your Website

Some people argue that on the web a blog alone will suffice. You need a blog and a website. Today they are usually connected and integrated, but they serve different functions. Your website will tend to be updated less and appear more corporate and polished. People will visit it to gather specific information about your company profile and qualifications, or products and services. A guerrilla's website is a combination of a storefront, brochure, and lead-capture device. Above and beyond this, it's a credibility builder; all of your marketing, social media activities, and client engagement must eventually link back to and aggregate at your website. A guerrilla's website is her home base and headquarters from which she launches her guerrilla social media attacks. Your website is where your brand and positioning are consistently reinforced.

63. Forums

These threaded discussion sites or modules are great marketing tools. They are truly among the first social media and predate web browsers such as Firefox or Internet Explorer. The majority of content created on forums is created by the users, not the owners of the website. Forums are usually broken down by subject or topic. Many companies use them to help their customers collaboratively solve problems, ask questions, and share information on common areas of interest.

Guerrillas use forums to leverage the power of community to:

- Identify and solve customer service problems
- Create keyword-rich content that ranks high in search engines
- Communicate directly with customers and prospects
- Collaboratively create solutions, identify trends, and reinforce their brand
- Test market ideas, campaigns, or concepts
- Poll and gather data
- Research

64. Microsites

A microsite is a stand-alone site or section of a site that is uniquely branded and built for a specific product, service, promotion, event, or niche market. If you offer multiple products to multiple markets, they can often get lost on a big website or a blog as readers search for what they are looking for. Microsites are great tools for launching new products or for building relationships and communities with specific nano-markets.

A good example is a new book launch. Many progressive publishers will build a site or section of a site that is specific to that book. It will not have links to other books, corporate information, or anything else that could lead the visitor away from the core goal of the marketing: to sell those books. All of the information on the site is focused on the benefits of the book and who endorses the book, and usually includes multiple options for pathways to buy the product.

Some of the benefits of microsites are:

- They make it easy to track marketing results.
- People are less likely to get lost, confused, or abandon the site.
- They allow for specific branding and marketing focused in great depth on one product.
- They offer more freedom to experiment, because they are tied to the corporate brand, site, or blog.
- They often mean faster time-to-market; it's easier to build a small stand-alone site than integrate with a large complex corporate site.
- The domain name itself often reinforces the product or promotion vs. the company name.

65. Alltop.com

Alltop is described by co-founder Guy Kawasaki as "the online version of the magazine rack in your bookstore except that it has 900 subjects and is free." It organizes news and blog entries by subject, and gives you the five most current pieces from top websites and blogs. You also get a preview of each story.

Guerrillas need to constantly feed their community and connections with value added content. They also need to keep up to date with specific industries and niche markets to remain competitive. Alltop's always current and up-to-date news and blog feeds are a great source of guerrilla intelligence and content.

66. Your Blog

The term blog is an abbreviated or shortened term that refers to a weblog. In its simplest form a weblog is an online diary or log where you post your thoughts, personal feelings, and stories. Guerrillas tell stories because stories are not boring. From a marketing perspective, a blog is a site that is updated weekly or even daily with your personal brand story.

Your blog is your brand story headquarters. It is the best place to have conversations with the community. Why? Using a sports analogy, you have the home court advantage on your blog. As you interact with people who make comments on your blog, the content created actually adds to and deepens your positioning, and creates a very personal, approachable online environment.

A blog is not a place for polished press releases, sanitized marketing images, or highly edited and legally vetted information. Guerrillas use their blogs to contribute to the community, their customers, and prospects. Engaging bloggers are never too formal; they use the medium to share best practices, and express and reinforce their positioning, values, and core benefits. By doing this they create trust, credibility, and consent to market to people.

You can have a blog that is self hosted, such as yourblog name.com. Or you can use one of many blog software providers, build your blog using their system, and have an address such as yourblogname.WordPress.com.

67. WordPress.com

This site is a massive hub for a community of bloggers. Available in over 50 languages, several hundred thousand blog posts are added daily to the network. It is free to use. You can immediately have a site with an address like yourblogname.WordPress.com up and ready for blogging in less than ten minutes. It comes with multiple theme options, and if you're a little tech savvy, you can even customize and brand those themes. There are options to add widgets and plug-ins that allow you integrate tools like Flickr, Twitter, and even podcasts into your blog.

The blogs come with an integrated statistics system, an option to make them private (members only), and comment spam filters.

Your blog entries are also included in their global searchable database.

There are limitations to how much you can modify WordPress.com blogs, and their terms of service do limit the nature and type of advertising that you do with your blog. Aggressive marketers or people who make income off of systems like Google Adwords may be stopped or deleted by site administrators because blogger-initiated paid advertising is against the terms of service.

One big benefit to starting with a WordPress.com site is how easy it is to export and move your site to be hosted on your own domain using a self-hosted version of the WordPress.org software. When you're starting off and have no marketing budget or resources, this can be very helpful.

If your blog is for business purposes it is advisable to start with a fully branded self-hosted solution that is consistent with your positioning and corporate website. If your blog is more personal in nature, WordPress may be a good option.

WordPress Self-Hosted
Blog Sites and Weapons

WordPress is the most widely used internet publishing tool in the world. There are also thousands of marketing weapons that can be added to the WordPress system. In this section we will discuss the importance of a self-hosted blog and the core weapons and plug-ins you need to add to your blog.

68. WordPress.org (self-hosted blog)

This tool is a guerrilla-approved social media weapon. The most widely used and flexible blogging software in the world, WordPress is the platform of choice for bloggers and social media marketers globally. Major domain registration providers like GoDaddy.com and hosting companies like Bluehost.com provide one-click WordPress installation options for free with your hosting packages. These packages are reliable and cost as little as $5 per month for hosting.

There are literally tens of thousands of WordPress developers globally. Any major city will have dozens of reputable and affordable development companies and individuals that can help you design and build your blog. Because the software is open source, there is an army of WP developers building every imaginable plug-in, theme, and marketing add-on for WordPress. Most of these extensions are free, and many are extremely effective add-on guerrilla weapons.

69. WordPress Themes

Your WordPress blogging software is the engine that drives your blog. Your theme impacts the look, feel, branding, and user or visitor experience. Some themes can make your site look like a news or information portal, others are designed with paid advertisers in mind, and some are more e-commerce oriented. There are even themes designed specifically with marketing squeeze pages or video-driven sites. Guerrillas always start with their target market and business goals in mind and then choose a theme, rather than choosing based on looks alone.

There are a lot of beautiful themes out there that are free. If you use one, just be aware that there may be hundreds or even thousands of people with blogs that look like yours.

Professional and customizable theme packs can be purchased from a multitude of sources online. For a few hundred dollars you can have a theme designed specifically for your business matching your branding and fonts with a customized user interface based upon what you will be using your blog for.

A guerrilla social media marketer's blog theme has the following attributes:

- Matches your branding and fits your logo and corporate color scheme

- ➤ Easy-to-use navigation that makes it easy to find important information
- ➤ Is fast loading
- ➤ Is secure
- ➤ Supports widgets and plug-ins and requires very little technical knowledge to install them
- ➤ Is search engine friendly
- ➤ Easy to add additional pages, sections, and categories
- ➤ Has an easy-to-read and attractive page and paragraph structure

WordPress Plug-ins

Plug-ins enable much of the marketing power and social and community aspects of blogs. Almost anything you could dream of as an added functionality for your blog has already been built and is available on WordPress.org's "Extend" section under "Plug-ins." Following are a few must-have plug-ins for guerrillas:

70. All in One SEO

Although social media marketing is a powerful force, search engines are still the top referral sources for most blogs. The All in One SEO plug-in allows you to easily tweak and modify title tags, descriptions, and keywords for your blog posts. If you don't want to do the manual work of optimizing your blog entries, All in One SEO has an option to automatically do this for you. It will embed keywords, descriptions, and display title tags that will more accurately tell search engines what's on your blog than the standard WordPress software will.

71. Share This

If you want to really extend and promote yourself and your brand, you must make it easy to share the information and resources on your blog. The Share This plug-in takes seconds to install and activate on your blog. Once installed, with a click of a button your visitors can share your blog entries with their social networks and social media connections. Share This allows people to share favorite links and media with over 100 social media sites including Twitter, Facebook, Google Reader, Friendfeed, Digg, Stumbleupon, and many other major networks. Guerrillas make it easy for fans and customers to talk about them by making it easy to share and promote them.

72. Tweetthis

Tweetthis is a must-install plug-in. It prominently displays a "Tweet This" icon at the bottom of your blog posts. By clicking on the icon a link and a message are automatically posted to the reader's Twitter feed. Many people neglect to add this plug-in, expecting others to cut and paste the link to the url and add a description to the link. Making people work deters them from sharing and reduces the potential for your blog post to go viral. Some people argue that a plug-in like "Share This" is sufficient but what it lacks is the big easy-to-see, easy-to-click "TweetThis" button.

73. Google Sitemap Generator

This tool automatically generates an XML sitemap and notifies Google and a number of other search engine crawlers when you add pages or blog posts. It ensures that you will have the maximum number of pages possible indexed by Google, Bing, and Yahoo.

74. Powerpress

Podcasting and internet radio shows are incredible ways to expand your reach, gain new prospects, and retain customers. The Powerpress plug-in makes podcasting easy and iTunes-compatible. You are also able to track the success of your show using the optional analytics package.

75. Google Analytics Plug-ins

This plug-in integrates Google's leading analytics tools into every page of your blog. There are many versions. A key guerrilla social media marketing secret is measurement. This plug-in ensures that you can track campaigns, visitor behavior, popular keywords, and even integrate that tracking data into tools like salesforce.com's CRM tool.

76. WP-touch

The web is going more mobile everyday, and Apple creates some of the most popular mobile devices. The WP-touch plug-in automatically detects if someone is viewing your blog using an iPad, iPhone, or iPod Touch and pushes out a quick-loading, mobile, Apple friendly web page that is easy to browse and read.

77. WP-o-Matic

Your ability to distribute and aggregate content is vital. This plug-in allows you to pull content in from blogs or any other source that has an RSS feed. The content is then published on your blog as posts. WP-o-Matic even allows you to add categories and publish content to different sections of your site based on which RSS feed it came from. Many people who have multiple blogs use this tool to aggregate their entries into one main site or category. One important search engine optimization warning: Google doesn't like duplicate content and may penalize you for this. Make sure you use the customer header and footer option with the feeds you pull. This will ensure that the content varies from the original source and search engines do not downgrade you for copying content to multiple sites.

One last thought: Always make sure you have permission from or give proper attribution to anyone whose content you are aggregating.

78. Akismet

This is a mandatory plug-in. It stops comment spam on your blog. Comment spam can drown out real comments, hurt your search engine rankings, make you look unprofessional, and waste a lot of your time if you are moderating comments manually. Akismet learns what is spam over time, based upon what you flag as spam, but it also works off a global blacklist of spammers put together by the thousands of bloggers who report spammers daily. This plug-in will save you time and protect your home base and brand.

79. WP-to-Twitter

This is another guerrilla automation tool. When you publish a new post, this plug-in automatically publishes an update to Twitter, which saves you the time it usually takes to open up your Twitter account, type in the headline, and tweet it. It is a small task, but many people have multiple blogs they author and publish on. Over weeks or months it's a large time savings. Warning: people who only use WP-to-Twitter to create content on Twitter are soon labeled broadcasters who don't listen. Take the time to visit Twitter and have real conversations, even if some of your updates are automated.

80. WordPress.com Stats

This plug-in and system was created by the makers of the WordPress software. It's not as comprehensive as Google Analytics, but it does provide an easy-to-understand at-a-glance graph and report. You can quickly see who your most recent referrers were and what your most popular posts are for the day and week. From a convenience perspective, it allows you to see your stats within the WordPress admin dashboard, centralizing your information flow.

81. Commenting System

Blog comments are what make blogs a social platform. Comment functionality allows you to have conversations with the community you are building. Comments are also used by your visitors to communicate with each other. Those comments add depth to your posts. There are many WordPress plug-ins that have been designed to enhance the commenting experience. Many even integrate and aggregate comments made on Twitter or other blogs and connect them back into your blog posts. There are dozens and dozens of these plug-ins available, but here are the big three:

- → *Disqus*. Allows users to reply to each others' comments. It also has a community aspect that keeps score of an individual's conversations and contributions to the blogging community. Disqus integrates with Akismet to provide a very efficient spam-filtering system.
- → *IntenseDebate*. Allows multiple ways to login and make comments through Twitter, Facebook, OpenID, or your WordPress account ID. IntenseDebate is similar to Disqus in functionality. Based upon our testing and feedback from other social media marketers IntenseDebate is a good tool, but a little less intuitive with its user interface than Disqus.
- → *WordPress*. Every WordPress blog has commenting functionality built in. With every software update, it just seems to get better; in fact, third-party tools like Disqus and Intense Debate may no longer be needed soon.

82. CMS or Content Management System

This tool (if used correctly) takes the reins of power and innovation away from your tech team and puts them in your hands, the hands of a guerrilla marketer. In the past, if you wanted to update a web page, add a new section to your site, or post a video, you had to hire someone with technical expertise to do it for you. In most cases small changes that need to happen immediately can be delayed by technical support staff that do not have the same sense of urgency as the guerrilla. A content management system allows anyone with a web browser to edit, update, and add to a website. Most come with a WYSIWYG editor (What You See Is What You Get) that looks and feels like an online word processing document and is often as easy to use as well.

CMSs have been available for over a decade, and the industry has hundreds of players. To help you choose the right CMS for your business, here are six characteristics of a good CMS:

1. Creates search engine-friendly pages
2. Has multiple modules that can be added, such as blogs, shopping carts, forums, private pages, forms, community functionality, and social media plug-ins
3. Can be technically updated or supported by a multitude of inexpensive suppliers and vendors
4. Keeps up with the latest advancements in technology and web marketing
5. Is inexpensive to host (many proprietary CMS companies charge outrageous hosting fees)
6. Makes it easy for you to make changes to the look, feel, and navigation of the site

Based upon the above criteria, some of the web publishing tools that qualify would be WordPress, Joomla, Drupal, and Mambo. There are many lesser-known CMS tools out there. Just make sure you pick a technology that is both stable and has viable future support. Our advice: stick with these four. If you do go with a lesser-known CMS, make sure you do a lot of due diligence on the technology and financial stability of your provider.

83. Ubertor.com CMS (for Real Estate)

Video blogging has become a core guerrilla social media weapon for those in real estate. Ubertor has built its CMS specifically for highly sociable real estate professionals who want to engage with their community online using video or text blogging. It meets the six characteristics of a good CMS, but also has additional features that are standard with all of its sites. For one example, when the marketer uploads a video to his site, it is automatically distributed to YouTube, Viddler, and a multitude of other video sharing sites. Those uploads are also automatically posted to Twitter.

Almost monthly, Ubertor adds more social networking and social media features to its system. The added advantage is that the CSS (style sheet) is unlocked. With an unlocked CSS the look, branding, and navigation of the site can be edited by almost any web developer on the planet. If you're a guerrilla real estate agent, this might just be the CMS for you.

84. RSS Feeds

RSS stands for Really Simple Syndication. It's a technology that has been around for a while and has many amazing applications. It drives much of the content distribution online, and enables organizations like the Associated Press to get their message out to millions of news sites. It's also what enables sites like Technorati to keep current and up-to-date on millions of blogs.

In its simplest form, RSS is a file format that breaks content and embedded media down to a simple universal format that can be aggregated and republished on almost any platform, browser, or mobile device. Guerrillas use RSS technology to get their message out to multiple sites, directories, and networks. You can also use it to aggregate information, updates, events, and media all into one place for guerrilla intelligence and brand management purposes.

Every time you do a Twitter update, post a blog entry, or subscribe to someone's blog, RSS is working in the background. The great thing about RSS is that you don't need to truly understand its technology to have it work for you. It is, however, advisable that you study this technology enough to maximize its applications in your guerrilla social media marketing efforts.

85. FeedBlitz

FeedBlitz is a service that can turn your blog RSS feed into a newsletter. You can set it up so it sends daily, weekly, or real-time updates to your subscriber base. All you have to do is blog, and FeedBlitz will pull that information into its system, format it as an e-mail, and notify people of the new content. It also gives subscribers the option to get updates via Twitter; in this instance they would get a short message and a link prompting them to check out your latest blog post. The newsletter template can be completely customized. You can also send on-demand updates or promotions to your subscribers. This is a great option, but make sure you don't overstep the level of consent you have been given. Sending too many promotions and not enough value-added content can cost you valuable subscribers.

86. Yahoo Pipes

This tool does require some technical know-how, so it may not be for all guerrillas. It enables you to aggregate, organize, filter, and republish RSS feeds. You could, for instance, pair a geographic Twitter search term such as "skiing" with the region Telluride, Colorado, then do a Flickr search for "skiing Telluride." With Yahoo Pipes you can mash-up these two feeds together and then republish them to a website, blog, or as links in a Twitter feed. The ability to filter by search terms and combine multiple sources of content is a very useful way to create content and distribute it to multiple sites and networks.

87. Wikis

Websites driven by wiki technology are a form of content management. They are typically very minimalistic in their design features. A wiki allows anyone to create and edit pages, often even without registering. Wikipedia is the world's largest crowd-sourced information source and is completely run and updated by literally millions of volunteers.

Wikis have many powerful uses for guerrillas, including:

➤ *Business operations management.* You can completely replace cumbersome binders and training documents with an internal or private wiki. Whenever a staff member develops a new business process or solves a problem, it can be recorded for everyone to see. Other team members can also add to it as time goes on. For geographically dispersed teams, it's a great knowledge management tool. As a guerrilla manager, it's much better and more efficient to say "look on the wiki" for operations and service questions. It saves time and ensures a consistent approach because there is a visible history for people to reference. It also means that key business information is always available, even when you are on the beach in Hawaii.

→ *Customer-collaborated solutions.* Guerrillas harness the power of the crowd by getting their customers and communities to contribute content. With a public wiki your customers can collaborate on product developments and business solutions. This is a great alternative to paying customer service representatives or investing your own valuable time. Having a customer-driven wiki is a very important community-building and brand protection move. Companies like Apple have thousands of unofficial support wikis run by customers, but much of the information is outdated or incorrect. Guerrillas protect their brands by providing tools like wikis to the customer. If you don't, it is quite possible your customers will self-organize and hijack your brand.

→ *Community building.* If you owned an auto detailing company, you could build a wiki for classic car enthusiasts in your local community. Trust is a key element in getting consent to market and sell to people. By sponsoring the creation of this wiki, you would elevate yourself above other marketers and be seen as a community builder and manager. The idea in this instance is NOT to post specials or blast marketing at the community; instead, you could reward contributors and community managers with gift certificates and discounts. Then allow them to spread the good word about your company.

88. Yourname.com

If you don't own your name online, stop reading this. Then go to GoDaddy.com immediately and reserve your name. When customers search for information on you, having yourname.com will almost guarantee that they will find all of the important information that you want them to have. Your social graph or online profile and personal brand are just as important or even more important than your company brand. Protect and build upon it by owning your own name.

89. .tel

This is a new domain name extension but it's more than just another domain. Yourname.tel, Yourproduct.tel, and yourcompany.tel are vital guerrilla tools. A .tel domain is driven by a proprietary software that integrates a variety of smartphone and web-based applications. Embedded in the .tel are your contact details and key information. With a click of a button, your prospects can immediately download your contact information into their address book or cellular phone. George Moen, CEO of Blenz Coffee, has a business card with no phone numbers, addresses, or e-mail on it. It simply says George Moen.tel.

What the .tel network is building is the worlds' biggest phone book that dynamically integrates into websites and applications. Anytime you update your contact details in your .tel dashboard, it automatically updates all of the other sites and the smartphone applications. How many times have you been somewhere and forgot your business cards? Now you can simply tell people to visit yourname.tel, yourproduct.tel, or yourcompany.tel. Most people will find that easy to remember and easy to do.

90. Yourbrand.com

Before settling in on a company name, always search and make sure it's available. Today your company name is a core asset. As a guerrilla marketer, you must own YourBrand.com. Every tweet and link you post should reinforce your branding. Having a domain that is abbreviated, an acronym, or generic will not help you find a place in the customer's mind.

91. Yourproduct.com

Just like your company name, you must also own your product names online. This will help you dominate the search engine rankings. Guerrillas make their products and services easy to find and engage with online. When people tweet, post links on Facebook, and talk about your product, it will reinforce the product name in the mind of the consumer.

Light Blogging Tools

Light blogging tools are easy-to-launch, easy-to-use guerrilla social media weapons. They're great for redistributing content, sharing your thoughts, and even networking with others. They tend to be more casual and have fewer features than WordPress or different types of content management systems. Most serious bloggers will have a main WordPress blog and then a Posterous or Tumblr blog as well.

92. Tumblr

This blogging software is a mash-up of concepts; you can follow other bloggers on Tumblr almost like you would on Twitter. You can also post content via e-mail and send photos to your blog directly from your mobile phone. When you log into your main page, you see the most recent entries of those blogs you are subscribed to. Many people use Tumblr to re-blog content from other sources; you can pull multiple RSS feeds into your blog and create a mash-up of content from your main blog, Flickr, Twitter, and almost any other service that is RSS-driven. With a click of one button, you can repost blog entries by other Tumblr bloggers; this reposting function can help your content and marketing go viral. Tumblr also comes ready for podcasting and has free podcast hosting built in. With a little technical knowledge, it is also possible to host your Tumblr blog at yourdomain.com. Tumblr can be fully customized in terms of look and feel, and allows you to use your own themes or one of their many themes provided.

93. Posterous

Most people who use Posterous make the majority of their posts via e-mail. After you set up an account, you can e-mail text, photos, audio, and even videos to a designated Posterous e-mail account. Within a few minutes your post is live. The real advantage of this blogging tool is that highly mobile guerrillas can do almost all of their blogging on their smartphone from anywhere in the world. The one disadvantage is the lack of customization available in regards to the theme; you are basically stuck with one look.

Social Bookmarking

Social bookmarking sites can send literally hundreds or even thousands of additional visitors to your website. Social bookmarking is a process whereby users curate content, add links, add reviews, and vote on the quality of your blog posts, videos, photos, and web pages. Some of these sites have millions of active users. The benefit for the user is they can access content based upon interest or topic and see how other users have rated and reviewed it. These sites are basically human-created and ranked search engines and directories.

The four major sites to focus on are Digg, StumbleUpon, Redditt, and Del.icio.us. They all have slightly different interfaces and community functionality. The two biggest traffic generators are Digg and StumbleUpon. When your link gets popular on Digg, you tend to get an immediate and short-term boost of traffic. If many people or one influential person votes and reviews your link on StumbleUpon, you can also get an immediate surge of traffic, but it tends to produce more ongoing traffic over the long term than Digg does.

Digg Tribes and StumbleUpon Alliances

To get the most out of these social bookmarking communities, guerrillas use a community and contribution focus in their activities. People who only submit links to their own sites don't tend to do well in these communities. On StumbleUpon you can even be reported and banned as a spammer for doing this. The idea is to become a trusted source for good information and insights on a specific group of topics.

For every one link that you are rating, reviewing, or posting that is about your business, you should be sharing and voting on eight to ten community links or links unrelated to you directly. Guerrillas build the trust of the community by sharing valuable content; once this trust is established they begin to fan out and add friends and connections on the site. If you're adding a friend/connection, make sure you send a personal message along with your request. Let your new potential connection know why you think they're great.

As these relationships progress, guerrillas will reach out to their new connections and form more formal alliances. There are Digg tribes that can literally push the right Digg post to the front page of Digg and deliver thousands of visitors to your site. These relationships take time and effort to build, but they can be huge traffic generators.

Mobile- and Location-Based Tools

The web and all of its applications will continue to become more and more mobile. Mobile social networks and social media-enabled sites are growing at an almost exponential pace. For those marketers focusing on specific geographic locations, these tools can produce great return on investment. Users with phones with GPS can vote, comment, and check-in at specific business locations. They can also search to see who is nearby at that very moment and add them as connections or ask their advice about a specific local business.

94. Foursquare

This is one of the most popular location-based mobile applications. Its popularity has been driven by the gaming component of the application. If you check into a location like your favorite restaurant or electronics store enough times, FourSquare will award you the title of mayor. Many smart guerrilla businesses are offering prizes, coupons, discounts, and special deals to those that check in at their business. Users can also add tips and reviews of the business from their phone. If the users choose to enable Facebook and Twitter integration, they can also post their location to these networks for all of their connections to see. Expect to see FourSquare add more data and content through various partners in the near future.

One effective guerrilla social media strategy when using FourSquare is to connect with those people who check into your competitors' businesses. If you owned a coffee shop and were competing with a nearby Starbucks you could easily migrate customers from their location to yours. The FourSquare site lists everyone who checks into a business location and usually provides their Twitter address as well. By following these people, beginning a dialogue, and providing a special Twitter coupon, you could motivate many of them to frequent your business instead.

95. Brightkite

Similar in functionality to FourSquare but slightly less popular, this application has some interesting functionality. The Brightkite iPhone app helps to automate posting updates and photos to multiple networks. After snapping a photo you can upload it with a comment to Twitter, Facebook, and Flickr all at once. All photos and updates are tagged geographically and are posted along with an embedded Google Map of the location. On Brightkite.com, anyone can view comments and photos on a specific location or business. By running contests with customers and posting your own business photos and comments, you can create an ever-growing source of business information and pictures about your business.

96. Facebook Mobile

This Facebook application can be accessed through a mobile web browser. In the case of the iPhone and BlackBerry, you can download a specific application with more functionality than the browser-based version. It enables you to stay in contact with your network of Facebook connections while mobile-posting photos and updates from events or interesting places. Facebook mobile also allows you to manage your business's Facebook Pages, add friends, and check private messages, and it provides a phone book of all your connections' phone numbers that have been listed on their profiles. For the mobile guerrilla who is using Facebook as a marketing tool, this application will help you stay virtually connected and efficient from almost anywhere.

97. Qik

A video streaming tool that is highly mobile, Qik allows you to broadcast video in real time from over 140 different types of phones. As you record, it is uploaded to the Qik server. It can also broadcast in real time, and will let your friends and followers view and comment as the live broadcast is occurring. There are several social sharing options that can push your video automatically to your Facebook wall, Twitter, and YouTube. The system also allows you to make the videos private, in case you only want specific clients or people to view them. Guerrillas are always on and ready to capitalize on a social media marketing opportunity at any moment. Having the ability to broadcast your message or a newsworthy event to the world instantly is a key guerrilla tactic.

Guerrilla Intelligence Tools

Before planning a marketing attack, guerrillas gather intelligence. You need to survey the environment for opportunities and threats. In addition, guerrillas research their potential markets, customers, and competitors by using guerrilla intelligence tools. These tools allow you to pinpoint and listen to specific conversations, monitor people, and drill down to communities in specific geographic regions. These social media monitoring tools are your eyes and ears on the ground. Being able to sort through the noise and gather relevant information helps you deepen customer relationships and keep ahead of the competition.

> Once you find a conversation about your brand, encourage it to spread by creating and hosting places for dialogue. Social listening strategy comes before social media content strategy.

98. search.twitter.com

This is possibly the most important search site on the internet. With close to 100 million users, you have a massive pool of up-to-the-minute conversations happening globally. When searching for information about a region or industry, Twitter Search provides something different from that provided by search engines like Google, Bing, or Yahoo. Instead of organizing information based upon algorithms and computer crawlers, Twitter Search provides access to real human beings' thoughts. In addition, once you find people who are talking about your area of interest, you can engage them in real time on a very personal level. With the advanced search functions you can get very specific, pinpointed information. You can find the advanced Twitter search options by going to search.twitter.com and clicking on the "Advanced" option.

Twitter advanced search functions include:

→ Words

- · All of these words: Search for a tweet containing a number of different words
- · This exact phrase: Search for a specific phrase
- · Any of these words: Search for Tweets containing all or some of a number of different words
- · None of these words: Search but exclude specific words
- · By hashtag: A hashtag is a term with a # in front of it such as #marketing. People will often tag a tweet by topic using a hashtag, so you can search to see specific tweets tagged with that term

➤ Language: Search for tweets in over 20 different languages

➤ People
- · From a specific person: Search for tweets by a specific person
- · To a specific person: Search for tweets to a specific person
- · Referencing a specific person: Search for tweet that have mentioned a specific person

➤ Within a specific distance of a city, province, state, or region

➤ Dates
- · Since a specific date
- · Until a specific date

➤ Attitudes
- · Positive attitude :)
- · Negative attitude :(
- · Asking a question?

➤ Containing links

➤ Including retweets

How Guerrillas Use Twitter Search to Find and Engage Customers

Imagine you've just opened a brand-new children's clothing store in Portland, Oregon. There will be dozens or even hundreds of parents tweeting about children and family-orientated things. This is your target market: parents who are passionate about their kids.

Using the advanced search function, you could search for:

Any of the words: children, children's, kid, kids, son, daughter, niece, grandchild, grandchildren, granddaughter, grandchildren

Near: Portland (25 miles)

Time: In the past seven days

This would output a series of conversations; a portion of those conversations will be people are in your target market. Your next step would be to follow those people, and eventually engage them in dialogue. They will most likely follow you (if you're adding value) and thus learn more about you and your new store. These relationships can be leveraged through promotions, special offers, or even by a personal visit or special event. If you did this every day for 30 days and only found 10 new connections, you would have at least 300 people identified as potential future customers.

99. Twitter Grader

Twitter Grader ranks the top people on Twitter by geographic location. It uses an algorithm that looks at your number of followers and how many people you follow, and also takes into consideration the number of conversations and retweets you have. Based upon this, Twitter Grader ranks people from 0 to 100 percent. It's not foolproof, but this tool is one of the best ways for you to identify the most influential people in a city or region who are on Twitter (twitter .grader.com).

100. backtype.com

A lot of the conversation by your target market happens in blog comments, Twitter, and even sites like Amazon.com. These are valuable conversations and backytpe.com indexes this dialogue. This is a real-time, conversational search engine that indexes millions of conversations from blogs, social networks, and media, allowing you to keep up with the most current buzz on a topic.

101. backtweets.com

This service tells you who on Twitter is linking to a website with their tweets. When using Twitter Search to monitor your brand or your competitor's brand, you will miss the links that use url shorteners. Most people use url shorteners when linking to a blog or site in a tweet. Backtweets.com crawls through all of the shortened tweets to see what the true sites are that are being linked to. This important for two major reasons:

1. It gives you a much more accurate picture of the volume, nature, and sentiment of the conversations about any website.
2. It helps you identify members or potential members of your community that are supporting you and your marketing efforts.

102. Twellow.com

Twellow is the world's largest and most detailed Twitter business directory. Within North America, parts of Europe, and Australia, you can drill down to individual cities and regions to find the Twitter users in those regions. You can also search by keyword and geography, pinpointing people with specific words in their bio and a city, state, province, or region.

What is great about Twellow is that it's an efficient way to manually find new and interesting people to follow. Twellow is fully integrated into the Twitter API. That means you don't have to leave Twellow to follow people, you just click on the follow button beside their name.

The site also has a follower and following management tool. What it does is tell you who is following you and indicates whether or not you are following them. It does the same thing for the list of people that you follow. This can be a good tool to help you pare down and focus your list.

How Guerrillas Use a Tool Like
Twellow for Global Marketing

Imagine that you are a business consultant who specializes in improving the profitability of high-tech companies. Then imagine that you are heading to a new market to meet with your first client there. Ideally you would have more than one client in this region, making your travels there more profitable. Using Twellow, you can search for high-tech industry-related terms and business names within that specific region. You can then connect with those people and begin to foster a relationship.

Guerrillas plant seeds well before they harvest. Start researching new markets many months before you arrive. Use that time to build trust with your new connections and gain consent to take the relationship to the next step. This next step will be an in-person meeting or a group Tweetup (a meeting of people from Twitter) when you arrive in the city.

103. PostRank

A great overview of the active blogs on the internet. Postrank rates sites based upon their level engagement in numerous categories. Enagement level is calculated based upon how many social mentions have been via blog comments, Twitter, and social bookmarking sites about each blog post on the site. This can give you some very good intelligence such as:

- ➤ How you rank in comparison to competitive blogs
- ➤ Which types of blog posts are the most engaging on your site and your competitors
- ➤ Which types of sites and genres of blogs get the most comments and mentions by people online

104. Radian6

Arguably the leader in providing enterprise class social media monitoring tools, Radian6 is well recognized and endorsed by marketers, analysts, and influential tech bloggers globally. Some of the major capabilities of Radian6 are:

- → *In-depth and flexible analytics.* Their analytics are broken down into categories such as reach, sentiment (by positive or negative review), engagement, links to your site, plus comments and votes. Results can be filtered and broken down by language, region, or specific sites.
- → *Far-reaching guerrilla intelligence.* This system monitors over 100 million social destinations, including blogs, comments, video, forums, pictures, public data groups, and micro blogs like Twitter in real time. Well-aggregated, its reports are easy to analyze and use.
- → *Influence analysis.* Guerrillas measure influence differently; their criteria will be based upon their business goals or marketing campaign. This tool allows you to set the criteria for who and what is influential. It even breaks down community leaders or influencers by channel or social media type. By providing this customized profile and list of key influencers, Radian6 allows you to focus on engaging bloggers and social media influencers that will give you the highest return in investment.

    There is also the capability to integrate Radian6 with Sales force.com to help move leads and customers into a properly-organized sales and marketing pipeline.
- → *Guerrilla social media marketing management.* When working on large guerrilla social media marketing campaigns, you will be most likely working and collaborating with a team. Radian6 allows you to assign tasks, set up alerts, and monitor your team's progress and activity.

105. Attensity360 Community

This social media monitoring and engagement platform helps guerrilla social media marketers quickly glean actionable insights about their brand's social media health and engage as appropriate. With the Attensity360 listening platform, you can monitor and measure buzz around a particular brand and your competitors, helping quantify the impact of various social media activities and arming yourself with competitive intelligence. Attensity360's sentiment measurement platform helps you evaluate your brand health and your competitors' brand health over time. This tool helps drive a strong ROI from social media marketing by easily zeroing in on the channel that produces the most buzz. Attensity360 covers blogs, microblogs, discussion forums and boards, online news, Google Buzz, photo sites, and online video.

Using Attensity360 you can zero in on the most influential bloggers and twitterers within a sector, helping them drive an effective influencer outreach campaign designed to increase buzz and positive word of mouth. At the same time, a community manager can help neutralize negative word of mouth by zeroing in on the largest social media liabilities. Attensity360 Community comes with a system of alerts and team workflows, which ensures that a busy guerrilla marketer never misses an important social media trigger event.

106. Twazzup.com

This real-time news platform provides a well-laid-out view of the buzz created on Twitter about any search term. It also indicates who the most influential people are and which are the most popular blogs, pictures, and videos that are related to the term. The search function is fast, intuitive, and easy to interact with. If you're looking for a quick at-a-glance view of your Twitter buzz and related media, this is a great tool.

107. PostRank Analytics (analytics.postrank.com)

This tool is a paid service but well worth the investment. It rates each of your blog posts based upon user engagement. Integrated with

Google Analytics, it shows both your traffic level to each blog post and the on-site and off-site level of engagement of each post.

Some of the social media and social mentions that Postrank watches are Twitter, blog links, blog comments, and major social bookmarking tools. Guerrillas are always measuring engagement and are perfecting the topic area, length, tone, and focus of their blogging. Being able to track which blog posts are most and least engaging can help you identify key trends and themes that your target market reacts to positively. Engagement leads to consent and consent leads to sales.

108. Payment Systems

Social media is an instant media full of instant gratification for the user. If you want instant feedback, send out a tweet. Someone will answer you. If you want to find out instantly what events your friends are attending this week, look at Facebook events with one click. People want to buy when they want to buy; this means that guerrillas are able to take online payments instantly and easily. You must have a PayPal account as a bare minimum. It accepts all of the major credit cards and also takes direct payment from other PayPal account holders. As your business grows, ideally you should also have a credit card merchant account that is e-commerce ready. Guerrillas measure success by profits; make sure you maximize your profits by making it easy to pay you.

Directories

As we discussed earlier in the book, guerrillas make it easy to be found. Many directories now pull your blog RSS feed and republish your content on their site. This republishing provides additional opportunities for people to stumble across your message. In many cases they are also good for search engine optimization. Directories are also great for finding niche markets and people with specific interests.

109. Blog Directories

There are dozens of well-established blog directories on the internet. A quick Google search for "blog directory" will produce pages and pages of results. Some directories are highly professional, and all submissions to be included are vetted manually by an administrator. Other directories accept automatic submissions and don't edit who's included in their directory. Remember, you're judged by the company you keep, so only submit your blog to directories that will improve your profile and visibility.

110. Podcast Directories

Very similar to blog directories, podcast directories include thousands or tens of thousands of podcasts. Some even pull in the MP3 files, allowing people to play your podcast within the directory. Both the podcast and blog directories also have another guerrilla marketing application: they are great resources to find other guerrillas and influencers who make good partners and alliances. A great way to expand your podcast's listener base is to invite other hosts and podcast producers onto your show as guests. They will often promote the show to their list and community. Being a guest on their show will also increase your profile and exposure.

111. iTunes

The biggest music store in the world also has the highest quality and largest podcast directory in the world built in. Being listed on iTunes means that anyone who uses iTunes can directly download your show into their computer, iPod, or iPhone (and any other iTunes compatible Podcatcher/MP3 player). After you have produced a few months of shows, you can apply to be listed. Once approved, any future podcasts that you produce will automatically be listed with iTunes. Applying to be listed is as simple as clicking on the button that says "submit a podcast" in the podcasting section of your iTunes software on your Mac or PC.

112. Twitter Directories

Many people will look to Twitter directories to tell them whom they should follow. New directories are popping up daily. Take some time and research what directories would be relevant for you. The major directories are Klout.com, Twellow.com, Twibes.com, wefollow.com, and Twitterholic.com. Take some time to get listed under categories and tags that your potential clients and alliances would use to search for your products or services. As you gain influence, your profile on these directories will increase and so will the number of connections you gain.

Google Weapons

Google is that 800-pound gorilla of the internet, and every week it spins off more web-based applications and tools. Many people just use Google as a search engine, but that's only the beginning. There are literally more than 100 major applications and sites owned by Google. Following are the top ones for guerrillas.

113. Google Apps

Guerrillas are always looking for ways to be completely mobile while also secure and competitive. Google Apps provides a complete suite of tools and software that is platform and computer agnostic. Historically you would have your documents and e-mail physically stored on your computer. Office software costing hundreds or thousands of dollars a year was also on the desktop. Most also required constant upgrades, often demanding expensive IT support as well. Google provides many important office utilities for $50 per month per user; the only software you need is a web browser. Everything is stored on Google's secure, robust servers. In addition, you are not tied to any particular computer to access important documents, files, and the company intranet. Some of the major applications are:

- *Gmail for business.* A robust version of its free webmail, it has fantastic security, 99.9 percent uptime, and an incredible amount of storage.
- *Google Calendar.* A comprehensive set of calendar and agenda management tools, it allows scheduling, sharing of online calendars, and a utility for synchronizing your calendar with multiple applications, computers, and mobile devices.
- *Google Docs Documents.* A replacement for software like Microsoft Office, it includes spreadsheets, word-processing, and presentation software. There are many collaboration and publishing options available as well. You can share the document with another person, your whole team, or the entire world.
- *Google Groups.* These user-created groups are part forum, part e-mail list manager. They're fantastic for collaborating privately with a group of people and can also be public, acting almost like a forum.
- *Google Sites Secure.* This tool allows you to create web pages for intranets and group sites. Many guerrillas are using this tool to build internal company wikis and online training manuals and tools for their staff and partners. Because it integrates so well with the other Google tools, it makes sharing, collaboration, and communication very easy.
- *Google Video.* This is a very secure and private hosted video sharing tool. Great for posting training content, technical videos, or private announcements that you only want to share with your staff or partners.

With these tools you can cut costs, increase mobility, and decrease dependency on any particular computer or mobile device.

114. Google Profiles

Google Profiles provides an additional opportunity for you to create a presence online by becoming part of Google's searchable profiles database. As it rolls out more social networking tools to the marketplace, expect your Google Profile to become an important social networking destination. Google Profiles is also your Google Buzz profile page.

115. Google Friend Connect

A social network that can integrate with any website, it allows users of a website to see who else is a fan of that site and then allows them to interact, share information, and leave comments. It is one of the fastest ways to take a static website and enable it socially. It also allows you, the site owner, to interact with visitors, ask questions, and develop a deeper understanding of them. By also getting your own personal Google Friend Connect account, you can bring traffic to your site from other sites. You simply visit other sites that cater to the same target market as yours does, and connect and interact with them. Once you have developed a relationship based upon trust and consent, you can direct some of these people to your Google Friend Connect community.

116. Google Wave

Often referred to as a hybrid of instant messaging and e-mail, this social media application has many uses. It can be used for mini-projects, events, or collaborative problem solving with your team. It displays people's updates in real time as they type, which is one of the differences between Google Wave and Google Docs. It has hundreds of plug-ins that allow you to do everything from publicly sharing your Wave to embedding video conferencing right into it. This tool could also be considered a guerrilla intelligence tool because you can search millions of conversations for key terms related to your business or target market.

117. Google Alerts

Another Google guerrilla social media intelligence tool, Google Alerts provides the most up-to-date information on specific topics globally. By entering keywords like "wedding" or "getting married," an online bridal registry company could use Google Alerts to identify new blog entries, web pages, and even Twitter updates that indicate a need for its service or a potential online partner. Google's robots crawl and index millions of websites and RSS feeds daily. Every time a website is updated and Google finds new content related to your search, Google Alerts sends you an e-mail with a brief description and a link to the original site. You can also opt to subscribe to Google Alerts as an RSS feed.

Knowing when new and relevant information is posted is vital to guerrilla social media marketers. Being able to respond quickly, while an opportunity or topic is still hot, is vital to your success.

Key topics you must monitor with Google Alerts:

- ➤ Client names including both the company and key staff
- ➤ Competitor names including both the company and key staff
- ➤ Your company, service, and product names
- ➤ Your staff and team member names
- ➤ Key terms that relate to industry trends or events
- ➤ Keywords that indicate a need for a product or service:
    - · A hotel in Miami: "going to Miami"
    - · Authors and Speakers: "annual conference"
    - · Building Supply Company: "renovations"
    - · A Restaurant: "(Restaurant Name) + Review"
- ➤ Any search term combined with the name of a region to monitor specific mention of a topic in a certain city, region, or country

118. Google Feed Reader

This feed reader has dozens of social media applications. It allows you to pull blog RSS feeds into a dashboard and then organize them by categories that you create. Feed readers in general save you from visiting blogs to see if they have updates. Instead, you are simply notified when it happens, and you can usually read the entry from the dashboard. This alone can save you a significant amount of time. You can share interesting entries directly from your reader dashboard to Google Buzz and to your connections on Google Friend Connect.

Because tools like Twitter Search, Google Blog Search, and Back-Tweets.com offer search results as RSS feed, you can subscribe to common searches and review all of them from one dashboard. This is a great alternative to the time-wasting activity of retyping search terms and visiting multiple sites continually. If organized effectively, your saved social searches in your feed reader can work well as a social media monitoring tool.

119. Google Feed Bundles

Within Google Reader you can organize feeds into folders. These feeds can then be embedded as a widget publicly on a website or shared with specific people via e-mail. This enables you to redistribute your searches, favorite blogs, or several of your content sources via the feed bundle. You can also repurpose the feed on multiple platforms similar to the way Yahoo Pipes does.

120. Google Buzz

This social networking tool integrates with Google Chat, Google Profiles, Gmail, and Google Connect. It socializes and ties together many of Google's applications and allows you to connect with your contacts from multiple Google tools and some third-party social applications as well. Buzz is publicly searchable and combines the functionality of Friend Feed, Twitter, and forums but also can be delivered to your Gmail inbox like a threaded discussion in e-mail format. This is e-mail redesigned and made public, and has several applications for guerrillas:

> ➤ *Intelligence.* Search within the conversations and comments of millions of users.

➤ *Making new connections*. Connect with and engage other guerrillas with large amounts of feedback and influence on buzz.

➤ *Feedback and research*. Post questions, comments, and marketing information in Buzz and get feedback.

➤ *Private collaboration*. Select "private" as an option and invite specific people in for a sneak peek of a product launch or for feedback and collaboration.

E-Mail

Many people claim that e-mail is dead. This is far from the truth; in fact, e-mail drives an immense amount of traffic to websites, blogs, and social networks every day. With over a billion e-mail messages sent every 24 hours, this is a very powerful medium. It really qualifies as social media. It is bidirectional in nature and can be very personalized and specific. You can embed multiple media into an e-mail. Following are a few of the weapons guerrillas should be using in their e-mail marketing.

121. Your E-Mail Signature

This is one very overlooked guerrilla social media weapon. It's on the bottom of every e-mail you send, and often when people forward an e-mail they include the sender's signature. Your signature should include:

➤ Your full name
➤ Title
➤ Company name
➤ Website
➤ Blog
➤ Phone number
➤ Twitter ID (hyperlinked)
➤ Facebook Profile (hyperlink)

➤ Corporate Social Media Links (Facebook Pages, LinkedIn Groups etc.)

➤ iTunes Podcast Link (if applicable)

By providing these links, your e-mail recipient has more options to learn about you and interact through different media. The more media people interact with us, the more frequency of contact we have with them. The more contact we have, the greater the mind share and we gain. For example:

Shane Gibson
Author & Professional Speaker
Site: http://gmarketing.com
Blog: http://guerrillasocialmediaHQ.com
Tel: +1.604.351.5539
Twitter: @ShaneGibson
Facebook: http://Facebook.com/Author.Shane.Gibson
iTunes: http://tinyurl.com/sociablepodcast

122. E-Mail Newsletter

Offering free and exclusive content to your website visitors is a great way to gain consent and grow relationships. Have a prominently displayed form on your blog and website where your visitors can give you their e-mail address. Use exclusive and free content, white papers, studies, and special discounts as a means to motivate them to give you their e-mail and subscribe to your newsletter.

When writing your newsletter, keep it personable and stick to the formula of 90 percent value-added content and 10 percent pitch and marketing. If your subscribers are active readers of your blog and Twitter stream, your tone must be consistent across all platforms. Too many marketers get an e-mail subscriber and then send too many messages with too much marketing content in them. Guerrillas honor and respect the consent and trust they have gained from a subscriber. Vary your format to create contrast and keep interest between newsletters. One week send a link to a video and brief introduction, the next week send a four-part article. You can also use your newsletter to profile your latest YouTube video, blog entry, or recent Twitter buzz. Contrast, unique content, and targeted offers will help you convert community members into clients using newsletters.

Guerrillas are constantly measuring, testing, and streamlining their social media marketing strategy. This extends to e-mail as well. List management software like AWeber and Constant Contact host your list of newsletter subscribers and clients online. Some of the common features of list management software include:

- → *Analytics.* In-depth statistics on the behavior of your subscribers, including who opened the e-mail and what links they clicked. Most will also tell what time and date the newsletter was viewed or clicked on.
- → *Aggregation.* The ability to create lists and send varied messaging and offers to those with different interests, geographic region, etc.
- → *Campaign creation.* Once a person subscribes they get a series of pre-planned e-mails that are tailored to their interests or demographic.

List management software solutions help you convert prospects and community members into customers. You will also gain valuable guerrilla intelligence based upon how people consume and interact with the information you e-mail to them.

> While you were tweeting, your competitor got out from behind his computer and met with your potential client.

123. Event Marketing Tools

They don't call it social media for nothing! Social media is supposed to be social. Creating community, building stronger ties, and therefore more trust is a core guerrilla social media marketing mandate. Integrated marketing is the way to really get a return on investment from social media marketing. This means combining multiple media and marketing tactics, including real life events where you can connect with and deepen relationships with your online friends. Here are some tools that can help you transition your online relationships into real life, in-person interactions:

- → *Meetup.com*. For an annual fee Meetup.com provides a comprehensive suite of tools to help you promote your events. In addition, it is a social network. Members join and indicate what types of events and areas of interest appeal to them. Within their geographical region, they will be sent updates on matching events. As an organizer, anyone who's interests are in line with your groups topics will be notified. In addition to this, it is advisable that you notify your Twitter, Facebook, and LinkedIn connections about your group. If you organize a professional, value-added networking opportunity or seminar consistently, you will be almost guaranteed to grow your network and deepen relationships.

  > Meetup.com is best used for community events. Using it just to promote your product or company will have minimal results.

- → *Eventbrite*. If you want to charge for the events you hold, this tool is a great ticket-selling system. It integrates with PayPal, enabling anyone to take payment for their events. If your event is free, there is no cost to use Evenbrite as an RSVP system. For paid events, there is a small fee per transaction.
- → *Tweetup organizing sites*. Tweetups are casual events which are attended by people who are connected via Twitter. Many Tweetups are simply tweeted spur of the moment as a means to invite people nearby to meet in person. Sites like twtvite.com

provide a very easy-to-use Tweetup organizing solution. This is ideal for organizing larger events or when you need to know the number of people attending.

Weapons of the Very Near Future

Guerrillas observe the battle ground and are masters at being totally present and focused. They also have an eye on the horizon, looking for opportunities and new competitive advantages. By the time you read or hear about a new technology on CNN or even TechCrunch.com, it already has been put to use by forward-thinking guerrillas. There are dozens of new applications and technologies introduced daily to the marketplace. Here are three tools that are starting to have a big impact on the way we market.

> Use your experience in social media to predict areas of growth in new regions and niches. Often when you discover new media channels, you also discover new markets.

124. Augmented Reality Applications

Augmented reality is a technology that layers data, photos, media, and other information over your natural environment. Imagine holding up your iPhone and panning your environment with your video lens. As you look through the led display, information about the street you are viewing is added virtually. This layer of data could include:

- Which of your business contacts are in the immediate area
- Specials and deals from businesses you have selected to hear from
- Embedded holograms showing clothing and other items on people
- Virtual tour guides that will navigate you through a store or community

➤ Enhancement of a product, or business environment to give the visually impaired access to your marketing information

Major organizations such as Yahoo and Google are producing, testing, and using this technology successfully. There are also several iPhone applications that are beginning to make augmented reality extremely mobile. Some of these tools will also project an image of you into an artificial environment and allow you to interact with it. Xbox's Project Natal also uses a form of augmented reality. Expect video cameras, software, and low-cost tools for marketers to come into the marketplace soon, which will allow guerrillas to access this technology and to drive business from it.

125. Social CRM

CRM refers to customer relationship management software and is used by enterprises to keep track of client and prospect relationships and to drive their sales process. Social media, hyper connectivity, and the rapid pace of change in the marketplace has changed the way salespeople need to engage. Unfortunately, most are working off a 1990s playbook for sales strategy, and their CRM is also stuck in the '90s. In the past you would get someone's contact details and push messages at them, then follow up with frequent phone calls and direct mail, hoping to hit them at the right time with the right message. A lot of resources were wasted. The salesperson or marketer, who was expected to enter a lot of data and details about the prospect, would also have to constantly research and keep up to date with each prospect.

With social CRM your database or CRM is living and dynamic. Imagine meeting someone at a networking event. You enter their .tel address into your social CRM, and it pulls in all of their contact details along with information on social networks they are part of. Over a few days, weeks, or months you build stronger ties with this prospective client on Facebook, Twitter, and several other social networks. You also subscribe to his blog and join his corporate Face-book Page. Within your social CRM, you can pull all of the publicly available data on this contact (based upon the level of consent you have from them) into one place.

Every time your prospect posts a new blog entry or comments on his day on Twitter, that information is pulled into and stored in the CRM. With this information you can identify buying cycles, hobbies, personal information, and even his favorite food. This in-depth knowledge of the customer enables guerrillas to be highly engaging in their marketing efforts in a customized, relevant, and well-timed fashion.

126. Smartphone Payment Systems

This rapidly evolving payment option makes it easy for mobile guer-rillas to do business. While enterprise level mobile payment solu-tions have been available for over a decade, they have been too expensive for independent marketers and entrepreneurs to use. Now with SMS (cell phone text) payment options and new BlackBerry, iPhone, and Nokia payment tools being developed, almost anyone can take payment via a mobile phone. Two people with the iPhone PayPal App can now simply bump phones together to transfer pay-ment from one person's account to another. Squared is a mobile iPhone payment system that has just hit the market. For a few hun-dred dollars' set-up fee and a minimal ongoing management fee, you get a credit card swiping attachment for your phone and an account. Squared acts as your merchant credit card provider much like PayPal does. While the use of these tools is in their infancy, this method of convenient payment will allow almost anyone to provide credit card payment from almost anywhere in the world.

There you go! You now have a master's degree in guerrilla social media armament. You will not use all of these tools. In fact, we strongly advise you to use under 20 tools to start. You can then evaluate which ones are working and also identify new ones to experiment with. Throughout the rest of this book, we discuss how you will be using these tools to launch and sustain a guerrilla social media marketing attack.

CHAPTER 5

GUERRILLA ROI

One of the core differences between guerrilla social media marketers and other marketers is how they measure success. When asked about return-on-investment (ROI) from social media marketing, many will claim it's impossible to truly measure. Some will say that it's all about community and suggest measurement isn't necessary.

Guerrillas measure their success neither by awards from other marketers nor the amount of noise they create. Guerrillas measure success by the amount of net profit or net results they generate from their marketing activities. They don't care about revenues unless they are turning a profit. Your marketing budget should always be based upon a percentage of the net profit you expect to gain from your marketing attack.

> Most social media efforts are abandoned long before their results can be measured.

Sometimes it's not practical or relevant to measure ROI solely by profits created. Net results are positive actions or results that may not be directly monetary but affect your profitability or organization's overall success.

Some examples of net results are:

- → A nonprofit society looking to help more people in its community may measure success by the number of new people who reach out for help and support.
- → Your human resource department will not measure success by revenues directly. Its social media ROI may be based upon the number of qualified new job applicants.
- → A parenting meetup organizer's social media ROI would be measured by the number of new members who attend an event.
- → A customer service team could measure success by how many work hours the team saves through use of Twitter and a customer-driven service Wiki.

WHAT GETS MEASURED GETS IMPROVED

Anyone who says social media marketing can't be measured just plain doesn't get it. Social media is one of the most measurable platforms that has ever existed. Every Twitter update, blog post, Facebook link share, and YouTube video view is recorded and can be monitored with tools like Google Analytics. It is possible to know exactly which Facebook status update or link embed prompted a customer to eventually buy a product or service and what pages on your blog or website he viewed before doing so.

SalesForce.com can integrate with your website forms, Google Analytics, and the entire sales pipeline, and lead flow can be tracked from beginning to end. When a member of your sales team closes a deal that comes from a web lead, you will know what Twitter post or Facebook link originally prompted the visit to your site.

With tools like PostRank Analytics, Radian6, and Biz 360 you can also track the net increase of engagement based upon your social media activities overall. You can drill down and compare individual blog posts to see why one got more buzz than the other. By correlating information requests or e-mail subscriber patterns with engagement levels you can determine what content motivates your audience to give you greater levels of consent. You may, for instance, look at how many people subscribe to your newsletter or request additional information during a specific duration.

The importance of tracking with Google Analytics and using tools like Radian6 is that you can get direct and precise feedback on what works. This feedback allows you to learn how to improve your guerrilla marketing attack.

GUERRILLAS MEASURE ALONE AND TOGETHER

Each guerrilla social media weapon and action must be measured. Guerrillas measure both individual activities and the results of all of the combined social media marketing as well. Figure 5.1 is a hypothetical example of how Joe's Software measures its social media activity. Software Joe's approach will help him test and improve everything from how he writes individual headlines to what monthly social media topic or theme was the most engaging and profitable.

In many businesses there are results that need to be recorded and accounted for that may not be measurable by guerrilla intelligence

FIGURE 5.1
Joe's Software

Joe is using Twitter, Facebook Pages, blogging, and social bookmarking sites like Digg and StumbleUpon to engage his audience and drive traffic to his site.

With Twitter, Joe may measure:

- time of day that produces the most click-throughs.

- individual updates that got shared the most.

- posts that got the best click-through rates.

- posts resulting in the most forms filled out.

He could also compare what landing page designs people interacted with the most and what blogging post titles got the most votes on Digg and StumbleUpon.

Drilling down to individual tweets and blog posts in a larger campaign or marketing push allows Joe to tweak specific social media tool and actions. It also allows him to master the use of the weapons.

Joe also knows that using multiple social media tools at once increases engagement and buzz much faster than using one tool at a time. Naturally Joe will also measure the overall effectiveness of this activity by looking at increases in engagement levels, form submissions, traffic, and, of course, the sales that result.

tools. Imagine if someone sees your Twitter updates, joins your Facebook page, watches your videos online, and then physically walks into your business and makes a purchase. You may not be able to connect the activity directly with the result. Guerrillas use coupons, special offers, and incentives that ensure that people tell them where they heard about their business or promotion. This can make it easy for you to connect online marketing with offline results.

RETURN-ON-INVESTMENT

Guerrillas measure profit and net profitable action, not gross revenues or traffic. That said, there are many social media soft activities such as social banter on Twitter that eventually lead to hard results and returns on investment. It's important to note that guerrillas use gross profits, not gross revenues, in their ROI formulas. It's not how much money you make; it's how much you keep that builds a guerrilla lifestyle!

ROI happens in many ways. Many social media activities and results are community-oriented, reinforce your brand, and can't always be directly linked to a sale in the short term. Although not everything can be measured or accounted for, it's important for you to measure and quantify what you can.

Return on investment is a simple formula to calculate:

$$\text{(Gross Profits} - \text{Costs)} \div \text{Costs} = \text{ROI}$$

For instance, if Joe's Software invested 50 hours of employee time on a social media launch at an average hourly wage of $20 and generated $10,000 in gross sales with a 25 percent profit margin (a profit of $2,500), then the ROI would be:

$$(\$2,500 - \$1,000) \div \$1,000 = 1.5 \text{ times ROI}$$

That formula gives you a concept of how ROI can be measured, but your investment may not always be measured in time. Guerrillas dig deeper and use analytics and guerrilla intelligence tools to look at what core activities and conversations occurred during that time.

Joe could evaluate his return on investment from Twitter conversations by looking at the data he collected and then calculating the average ROI of a conversation. Joe's Software had 22 Twitter conversations with potential customers with an average time invested per conversation of five minutes or a total of one hour and 50 minutes. Joe's average hourly staff wage is $20. Thus the rounded up cost of tweeting was $40. Joe's Software did an average of five updates per conversation and one tweet per person included a link, totaling 22 links shared. Of those shared, ten were clicked on and four resulted in a gross sale of $399 each for a total of $1,596 with a profit margin of 25 percent or $399.

The ROI is:

$$(\$399.00 - \$40.00) \div \$40.00 = 8.75 \text{ times the investment}$$

We can also calculate the average profit on each activity leading up to the sales. A total profit of $349 would mean:

- ➤ 22 conversations were worth $15.86 per conversation
- ➤ 10 clicks from Twitter were worth an average of $34.90 per click
- ➤ 110 tweets were worth an average of $3.17 per tweet

It's important to note that the only way that this type of ROI can be achieved is if you engage as a true guerrilla. You can't just write headlines; they have to be great headlines. Your conversations on Twitter, Facebook, or any other network must be engaging, focused, and build trust.

If Joe had several employees tweeting, he could compare the profitability and ROI of each person's conversations and determine who on his team had the best approach. This insight could help his entire team increase its profitability.

Note: Joe's ability to calculate ROI would be based upon the analytics tools he used for link tracking and onsite activity and purchases. Google Analytics provides the ability to do this, and it's free.

20 TYPES OF GUERRILLA ROI

Although guerrillas know that profits are the number-one metric to measure success, they also know that there are many types of ROI that contribute to profitability but aren't always easy to quantify. These types of ROI include positively impacting the community,

finding great employees, and pinpointing better business intelligence. While
measuring your social media ROI, it's
important to take all of your net outcomes and results into account. Many of
these outcomes come as a result of your
contributing to and connecting with the
community. So here are the 20 different
types of guerrilla ROI.

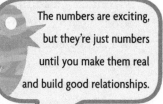

The numbers are exciting, but they're just numbers until you make them real and build good relationships.

1. Reputation

The more content you put out there and the more value you add to
the community, the stronger your reputation becomes. Reputation
is a key currency in social media marketing, and it increases everything from click-through rates to on-site conversions. Although reputation can't always be directly correlated to profits, it is a vital type
of social media ROI. Your reputation is built by providing a superior
customer experience and a great product service. It's also built by
your behavior as others observe your actions online.

2. Risk Reduction

Social media provides many types of risk reduction that can profitably impact your business. Being engaged and being involved
means that you will identify and react to threats or social media
attacks on your brand quickly, reducing the damage to your brand
and success. Another form of risk reduction comes from community. There is strength in numbers; with the fusion partners you create online, you can share marketing costs, and business intelligence,
and help defend each other's brands.

3. Client Retention

Providing value-added content and having multiple channels to connect with your clients increases the level of engagement and frequency

of contact. In addition, being connected with your clients on Facebook, Twitter, or LinkedIn can help you monitor their activities and sentiment, and identify opportunities to deepen the relationship and close deals. Companies that provide Facebook pages, Ning networks, Meetup groups, and client Wikis can greatly increase customer retention and therefore profits through engagement and trust building. Sometimes retaining a good client is a simple as quickly responding to a complaint about your business that it posted on Twitter.

4. Efficiency

Using social media and social networks to automate, crowdsource, and outsource business activities can greatly reduce costs and increase efficiency. As your network grows and your relationships deepen, you will be more efficient at researching, sharing your message, and driving traffic. Social media can save you time, effort, and money by leveraging your online community connections.

5. Business Intelligence

Guerrillas rely on intelligence to help them stay ahead of the competition, pinpoint opportunity, and plan their next wave of marketing attacks. By plugging into your online social media community, building alliances, and listening intently, you have access to important business intelligence from your community members and allies. Business intelligence can save you money, time, and effort, and help you make better business decisions.

6. Differentiation

Many guerrillas sell products similar to those of many competitors. In many cases the only differentiator between you and your competitor is your ability to establish meaningful relationships. You can also differentiate yourself by providing more value, education, and even entertainment to your target market. Investing in social networks in this way moves you from marketer and product peddler to trusted advisor and community member.

7. Brand Association

A brand is a promise that we keep or break with every interaction. A single Twitter update or an isolated blog comment doesn't seem much like branding activity. Yet collectively all of your tweets, comments, photos, and conversations tell a brand story. This story either keeps or breaks your promise. While competitors spend money on large short-term ad campaigns, guerrillas keep up the conversation with the community. You must keep up the conversation because that personal interaction over time strengthens your brand.

8. PR and Exposure

Something interesting happens when you're actively part of a community and contributing. Your social capital, reputation, and network all grow. Guerrillas know that if they position themselves in a community as a resource and trusted business connection, people begin to come to them for advice, insight, and direction. Many other guerrillas also refer their friends and business contacts to you. Being constantly connected and present also puts you top of mind with journalists and influential bloggers in the community. In addition, with a larger network and strong relationships, you increase the amount of buzz your message can generate.

9. Immediate Revenue

Guerrilla intelligence helps you pinpoint immediate business opportunities and prospective clients within your network. Most people you connect with online for the first time take time to increase consent and enter the sales cycle. Others, because of their situation or circumstance, are ready to do business today. The more active you are and the more connections you build, the more immediate business will be generated.

10. Long-Term Revenue

Consent to market to people and the depth of those relationships grows with your long-term presence in the community. Your blog readers, Twitter followers, and Facebook friends grow from fans to customers to advocates. Constantly adding value, delivering great products and services, and contributing to the success of others helps create an ongoing and steady stream of new and repeat business.

11. Supplier Capacity Building

For many guerrillas, finding new sources and new products or manufacturing partners is vital to their success. The challenge is locating new suppliers and then qualifying them. Your community and social network can help you find these contacts and often provide background information and personal reviews. This saves time and reduces the risk associated with dealing with new vendors or manufacturers.

12. Perception Shifting

Many people have a negative or incorrect perception of your brand, products, industry, or even personal character. Your involvement, conversations, and behavior on social media sites and social networks can shift the perception of those you interact with. Seemingly faceless large corporations who get human and connect intimately with these networks can warm up the chill surrounding their brand.

13. More and Better Recruits

People want more out of a career than just a paycheck. Today they want to be part of something significant and work with a company that has strong positive values and ethics. Another form of ROI in social media is the reduction in recruitment costs for your organization. Tools like LinkedIn, Twitter, Facebook, and industry-specific community networks give you direct access to new staff and talent.

Most of these recruitment tools are free or nearly free. In addition, your blog entries, Twitter activity, and other content you create attracts a specific group of applicants that resonate with your organizational values and brand.

14. Innovation

Innovative ideas can occur in many ways. For some it's a flash of brilliance while they're alone on a mountaintop. For many, innovative ideas are inspired by clients, competitors, or conversations that they have. Gathering business intelligence, interacting with different industry sectors, and working with other guerrillas online all can help you come up with innovative marketing concepts and solutions. Being able to interact with your customers in real time and spot trends and changes quickly is crucial for innovators.

15. Client Education

For many prospects, their lack of action comes down to lack of knowledge or understanding about the benefits of doing business with you. There is a large fear of the unknown that stops people from buying or even giving you consent to market to them. By providing comprehensive content, insight, and open channels of communication, you can educate clients about your business at their pace and in the medium they want. Additionally, tools like Meetup.com are great for getting potential customers on Twitter and Facebook into in-person meetings and educational events. The more knowledge that you and your customer have about each other, the greater your ROI will be.

16. Staff Capacity Building

It has been said that who you become in life has a lot to do with the people you have met and the books you have read. Today for many people it's the people they meet online and the blogs and media they consume daily. There is an unending amount of great educational materials and inspiring people on YouTube, Twitter, and the blogosphere. iTunes alone has thousands of hours of free business lessons from independent authors and universities that people can tap into. By getting involved in social media and social networks, your team has access to this content. In many cases it can also gain direct access to the authors and leaders that create the content.

17. Network Growth

One of the primary reasons people use tools like LinkedIn, Facebook, or Twitter is the social media and social networks that allow them to rapidly grow their network. Guerrillas who understand their target niches purposefully expand their networks into those industry or consumer groups. Guerrillas also create great value and content that is focused on their core target markets. This focus drives people to seek you out and connect with you through multiple channels. It takes time and money to grow your network. Social media if used effectively is an efficient means of doing this quickly and with a laser focus.

18. Opportunity Creation

Amazing things happen when you put a group of intelligent people together and allow them to talk freely and interact. Ideas emerge, partnerships form, and people are connected and referred to other people. Social media platforms and sites can sometimes resemble online versions of cocktail parties and networking events. Guerrillas know to take the time to be social with the right people. Through great dialogue and conversations many business opportunities and alliances can be created.

19. Job Satisfaction

Today's employee is hyper-connected; many prefer to text people or interact via Facebook than to pick up the phone. People don't want to be isolated in their cubicle; they're used to having access to a broader community via social networks. Creating opportunities for your team to positively interact, collaborate, and express themselves using social media can add a new level of satisfaction in the workplace. This increased connectivity, if channeled correctly, can also help your team collaboratively solve problems and efficiently interact with customers.

20. Trust Building

Social media allows you to let many parts of yourself and your business organization become visible and transparent. This openness and authenticity makes the community and the consumer feel confident and safe in dealing with you. Being present continually in the online communities you are involved in creates familiarity, and familiarity breeds trust. Trust and credibility are, of course, the key ingredients in making a sale that leads to a long-term profitable customer.

PUTTING IT ALL TOGETHER

There are both linear and nonlinear paths to ROI in social media. Guerrillas measure and account for both. Building a foundation of trust, community, and credibility with your customers and prospects ultimately leads to better response rates and repeat business. You can track how many clicks a link gets and how many of those lead to a sale. You can't always track the smile a blog entry puts on someone's face or the increase in trust that your latest video created.

Guerrillas use a series of soft steps to build a relationship that increases consent and eventually leads to a lifelong customer. These soft steps include free reports, webinars, hosted networking functions, commenting on other people's blogs, and promoting your prospects business online. Other soft steps may simply be taking the time to have a dialogue with some Twitter followers about an area of common interest. All of these activities build community and may not be seen as direct marketing investments, but they create strong relationships and the return on strong relationships in business is very high.

The guerrilla conundrum is that you always measure success in profits but you generate those profits by using strong intentional relationship-building strategies. When you measure the number of tweets it took to get a click-through, you must also be very honest about how authentic and relevant each update was as well. Never post a tweet, write a blog entry, or publish a video unless it truly adds value and genuinely helps your audience. Your intent and quality of content and conversation drives your return on investment much more than the volume or level of noise in your social media marketing.

You need to record the time, energy, and money invested in your social media activities monthly. You then need to record the volume of traffic, clicks, and revenues generated. In addition, you record any profit, cost saving, or net results that have occurred in any of the 20 types of ROI that have been discussed. Focusing solely on your level of engagement and ignoring your level of profitability will cause you to be a very popular but most likely broke marketer. Only focusing on blasting messages and short-term results almost ensure you short-term success and long-term losses.

Figures 5.2 and 5.3 are two ROI calculation templates. One has been completed as an example, and the other has been left blank for your use.

FINAL THOUGHTS ON SOCIAL MEDIA ROI

The example included in Figure 5.2 is a one-month snapshot. The reality is that most successful marketing campaigns in social media or traditional media take time to prove ROI. It is good to keep score monthly and also important to measure individual promotions. It is equally important to stick with your well-thought-out marketing

FIGURE 5.2

Joe's Software Guerrilla ROI for March

Weapons	Hours x Cost Invested	Cash Invested	Net Savings	Gross Profit
Twitter	15 x $20 = $300			$1,000
Facebook Page	5 x $20 = $100	$1,000		$500
YouTube	6 x $20 = $120	$200		$400
Digg	4 x $20 = $80			
StumbleUpon	4 x $20 = $80			
Google Buzz	5 x $20 = $100			
Blog	12 x $20 = $240	$1,500		$2,000
Meetup Event	20 x $20 = $200			$500
Tweetups	5 x $20 = $100			
	A = $1,320	B = $2,700		

Additional Types of ROI Realized:	How Was It Realized?	Net Savings	Gross Profit
Client Retention	Solved complaints and problems using Twitter	$2,000	
Recruitment	3 candidates and 1 hire with no advertising	$500	
PR and Exposure	Blog resulted in full-page newspaper article	$2,000	
Total:		C = $2,500	D = $6,400

FIGURE 5.2

Joe's Software Guerrilla ROI for March, continued

C $2,500 + D $6,400 = $8,900 (Gross Profit)

A $1,320 + B $2,700 = $4,020 (Cost)

$8,900 – $4,020 (Net Profit) ÷ $4,020 = ROI of 1.21

This month's net profit = $4,880

This month's ROI = 1.21

FIGURE 5.3

ROI Calculation Worksheet

Weapons	Hours x Cost Invested	Cash Invested	Net Savings	Gross Profit
	A =	B =		

FIGURE 5.3

ROI Calculation Worksheet, continued

Additional Types of ROI Realized:	How Was It Realized?	Net Savings	Gross Profit
Total:		C =	D =

C _____ + D _____ = _____ (Gross Profit)

A _____ + B _____ = _____ (Cost)

Gross Profit − Cost (Net Profit) ÷ Cost = ROI

This month's net profit =

This month's ROI =

plan and guerrilla marketing attack for months, possibly even years. All of the hard work in launching a new blog and building a Twitter following can take time to show the true and total ROI. The data you gather monthly should be compared month-to-month, quarterly, and yearly to track your progress.

> Integrate your tools in your marketing but also measure the effectiveness of each tool individually.

One of the biggest marketing costs isn't bad ideas, it's abandoning good ideas too soon. Mediocre marketing done consistently over time will beat inconsistent brilliant marketing every time. Use your measurement to fine-tune your approach and resist the temptation to change directions too often.

CHAPTER 6

GUERRILLA
FOCUS

Guerrillas know that every action must be purpose driven and part of a bigger strategic plan. As Fred Shadian says, "When mission is clear, abundance will appear." This quote resonates with the fundamental principle of *Guerrilla Social Media Marketing*, the power of focus.

Being able to clearly define goals, markets, and target prospects is vital. You must also be consistently focused on creating a strong brand and presence by carefully concentrating on the right content creation, conversations, and messaging.

If Facebook were a country, it would be the third most populous in the world. Marketing your business on Facebook without a focused profile of your ideal customer means that most of your efforts and money invested will be wasted. The same holds true for Twitter. In order to begin valuable conversations that build relationships with profitable customers, you need a very detailed profile of your ideal customer to sort through the tens of millions of social media profiles.

Your success in engaging people greatly relies upon you truly understanding your customers, their core values, and needs. Focusing on a specific target market and studying it at great depth gives you the insight you need to have relevant and valuable conversations. They also allow you to craft blog entries, and create videos and status updates that appeal directly to the needs, values, and goals of your target market.

Creativity isn't magic, nor is it something possessed by only a few people. Everyone, if disciplined enough, can become creative. Creativity actually comes from knowledge: the more knowledgeable you are about your customer, the more creative you can get with your strategy to engage with them and gain consent.

IDENTIFY THE RIGHT TARGET MARKETS

This process of profiling your ideal customer has been adapted from Bill Gibson's *Targeting the Right Clients* (1997–2010 Knowledge Brokers International) process. This process has been used by everyone from major banks to automotive companies like BMW. Companies that have effectively implemented this process have been able to generate significant increases in sales totaling millions of dollars at times. We have now taken the process that Bill has used with sales and marketing organizations and have seen great results applying it to social media marketing.

All guerrillas have heard of the Pareto Principle: 80 percent of your business is going to come from 20 percent of your clients and prospects. Having targeting criteria and constantly fine-tuning that criteria ensures that you are making a profit and continually growing your profit margins.

> All of your energy, resources, and social media activity should be focused on your most profitable clients and prospects. You need to be able to identify and quantify these markets.

Follow these steps to develop your ideal client profile:

1. Brainstorm all the possible criteria that you could use to build a client profile.
2. Choose the top five to seven criteria from that list.
3. Develop a key identity statement for each of the five to seven criteria you have selected.
4. Identify nano-tribes within this target market profile to which you will be nano-casting.

BRAINSTORM CRITERIA

In this step you will list all the possible criteria you will use to build your ideal client profile. Don't worry if they're right or wrong or which one's best while you're brainstorming. Just list at least 25 criteria that pop into your mind first, and let it flow freely. Here are two lists of possible criteria when targeting consumers and businesses. These lists are followed by Figure 6.1, where you can brainstorm your criteria.

Sample Consumer Criteria
- Age
- Gender

➤ Where they live
➤ Where they work
➤ Income
➤ Profession
➤ Hobbies
➤ Where they travel
➤ Number of children
➤ Blogs they read
➤ Use of social media
➤ Hours spent online
➤ Shopping habits
➤ Education
➤ Clubs and associations
➤ Social influence
➤ Value of their home
➤ Ages of children
➤ Political affiliations

Possible Business-to-Business Criteria

➤ Annual revenues
➤ Profitability
➤ Location of head office
➤ Number of offices, locations, or stores
➤ Number of staff
➤ Industry
➤ Social media presence
➤ Executive level of social media presence
➤ Amount of money spent on the types of products or services you offer
➤ Potential access to decision-makers
➤ Existing budget for your types of products or services
➤ Reputation
➤ Referral power

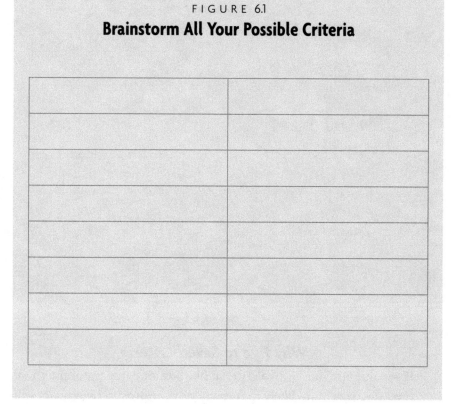

FIGURE 6.1
Brainstorm All Your Possible Criteria

Now that you have your list of possible criteria, it's time to choose the ones that are going to be most vital for you to identify your most profitable clients or prospects. Take a look at the lists and ask this very simple question: If I could only know one of these things about a customer, which one would be most helpful in identifying the profitable ones? List that as number one for your criteria in Figure 6.2. Then, ask that question again: if you could know just one more thing, which would be the most important to know out of all these criteria? Repeat this process until you've identified five to seven criteria.

FIGURE 6.2

Your Five to Seven Top Criteria

1. _____

2. _____

3. _____

4. _____

5. _____

6. _____

7. _____

Why Five to Seven Criteria

If we only use one or two criteria, like size of company and annual revenues, it is quite likely that many of your prospective clients will not be great fits. Size of company and annual revenues alone will not tell you enough to allow you to focus and direct an effective and relevant guerrilla social media marketing attack. On the other hand, having more than seven criteria will make profiling both overcomplicated and time-consuming. In addition, if customers meet your top five to seven criteria, in most cases they're already more than qualified. The additional information isn't typically needed to make a marketing decision.

Criteria Identity Statement

Your criteria identity statement is the foundation on which all of your guerrilla social media marketing strategies are based. It will drive who you monitor with guerrilla intelligence tools, what social media platforms and weapons you use, and how you communicate.

Let's take a look at a hypothetical guerrilla named Fred. Fred is a personal trainer living in Portland, Oregon. Following is a sample criteria identity statement for Fred.

Fred's Top Seven Criteria

1. Where they live
2. Profession
3. Health consciousness
4. Gender
5. Commitment to change
6. Referral power
7. Time

Fred's Criteria Identity Statement

1. *Where they live.* My clients live within a ten-minute drive of my gym.
2. *Profession.* They are professionals, executives, and independently wealthy entrepreneurs.
3. *Health consciousness.* They are very aware or desire to be aware of healthy eating and lifestyle choices and consider it a high priority in their life to improve and maintain good health through balanced eating and exercise.
4. *Gender.* My services and approach resonate more with men.
5. *Commitment to change.* My customers are highly motivated to make a change to improve their health.
6. *Referral power.* They are well-connected and networked with my ideal client market and are actively endorsing and promoting the products and services they love online.
7. *Time.* My customers have busy schedules, but do have sufficient time to devote to their health regimen.

FIGURE 6.3

Criteria Identity Statements

1. _____

2. _____

3. _____

4. _____

5. _____

6. _____

7. _____

Take your five to seven criteria and transfer them to Figure 6.3 and write down your criteria identity statements.

Applications of Your Criteria

Having solid criteria will help you focus in many ways. When looking at which online communities, social networking platforms, or even events that you're going to attend offline, having solid criteria can be very helpful. Before you choose to join a social network, take a look at its member base and the average user and compare that to your criteria. Focus on the networks with the highest concentration of people or companies that meet your criteria. If you have an online advertising budget, use your criteria to audit your existing advertising and cut out the sites with a low concentration of visitors in your target market. Also use it to seek out other businesses and develop alliances and partnerships with those who cater to your client market specifically.

Have you ever had a, "Gee, thanks," lead? You've probably never said it directly to the referrer, but inside most of us have thought, "Gee, thanks for that horrible lead. That's not my ideal client at all." This isn't the fault of the referrer. He's obviously enthusiastic about your business and wants to help you. The challenge in this case is that you have failed to focus the mind of that person giving you the lead. When someone says to you, "I may have a potential client for you," quickly respond and say, "Fantastic! Let me tell you about my ideal client!" By sharing your criteria with your referral source, it'll help focus his mind and identify possible prospects that may not have even previously occurred to him.

NANO-TARGETING

*"The problem with social media is that it is
1,000 people wide and two inches deep."*
—Malcolm Gladwell

Brand revolutions don't occur by casually marketing to thousands of people. They happen by intensely focusing on a small specific group of customers and turning them into loyal advocates. In the past we would choose a large target market and then generically blast messages at a specific but large group. Niche marketing then came along, which meant focusing on a more distinctive market, becoming a specialist, or developing custom products for large groups of people.

> Aggregate your client and prospect list, and develop nano-casts for each nano-segment.

In social media, nano-casting strategies are the guerrilla marketers' key strategy tool. With social media marketing the idea is to focus on small communities that are intimately connected and collaborative. By tapping into these nano-tribes, we can then do more than market, we can connect at a deep personal level and win over our target prospects in a way that our competitors can't.

Some examples of nano-targeting would be:

- A coffee shop targeting Twitter users who check in to coffee shops on FourSquare more than five times a week within one mile of its location
- A fitness club building a community site specifically for members who are skiers to swap health and training tips with one another
- An independent Apple retailer targeting nature photographers who are Macbook Pro owners working in the downtown area of a major city

Carrying on with our example from Fred, he could identify nano-markets within his specific client niche and build a series of separate blogs that cater to each. He could have one blog for people trying to lose those extra pounds, another blog for active athletes who want better conditioning, and yet another one for executives who are getting back in shape after an injury or illness. By developing blogs catering to those nano-markets, Fred will develop a much more intimate relationship with his prospects and clients by creating content and conversations that speak to their specific needs. In addition, those people who visit the sites receive additional value by being able to connect with one another. This is much more powerful than developing a generic, broad-topic fitness blog that doesn't speak to anyone's individual needs.

Nanocast to many small niches instead of broadcasting to everyone.

Reflecting on the above examples, think about the types of nano-markets and nano-communities that you could build or tap

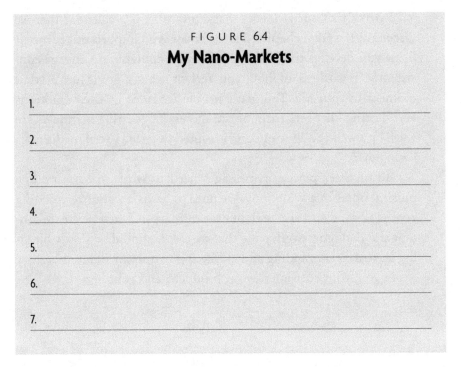

FIGURE 6.4

My Nano-Markets

1. _____

2. _____

3. _____

4. _____

5. _____

6. _____

7. _____

into within your target market. In Figure 6.4, list and describe five to ten lucrative nano-markets within your target market, and describe them in detail. The more specific you can get about your nano-markets, the more creative and engaging you can become in your content and dialogue.

Focused Social Media

There are a lot of places in the social web where we can create content. We can blog, Twitter, share things on Facebook, run contests and promotions, submit articles to portals, and create discussions on LinkedIn. Guerrillas stay focused by having a solid social media marketing plan and sticking to the plan. Being focused also means we don't get distracted by flavor-of-the-month technology or topics and concepts that are irrelevant or off-message for your brand and community.

Part of that social media marketing plan is a calendar that we discuss in the final chapter. The calendar is so important because it helps you develop the discipline to create content and engage consistently, regardless of how you feel or what's going on at that moment in your life. Too many people are ruled by their emotions and fleeting knee-jerk inspiration; successful guerrilla marketers are ruled by a well-thought-out and executed guerrilla social media marketing plan.

All of these pieces or messages need to work to together like musical notes in a symphony. We need to focus on our overreaching goal as a brand and also with our target markets when we create content and dialogue. Every piece that we create should be slowly building up to a clear branding and marketing symphony that tells a story about you, your customers, your products, and your brand.

CHAPTER 7

GUERRILLA SOCIAL MEDIA MARKETING DEFINED

Guerrilla marketing in its purest form is about achieving conventional goals using unconventional means. There are a lot of people using social media as a marketing tool, but many are still approaching it as if it were a conventional marketing media. They're spending a lot time, energy, and resources blasting out content, pitches, and generic marketing slogans and offers. Guerrilla social media marketing is about being ROI-focused and leveraging the time invested in marketing activities. You leverage your investment

> Guerrilla marketing is about achieving conventional goals using unconventional means. Instead of large sums of money your weapons are information, imagination, innovation, and community.

by combining your time, energy, and money with innovation, imagination, and community contribution.

What you lack in resources you must make up in resourcefulness. Even if you have a lot of money to invest, think like a guerrilla and look for smart ways to invest your time, energy, imagination, and information. Being able to achieve conventional goals by these unconventional means will give you a huge advantage over the competition.

Since the term "guerrilla marketing" was coined in 1984, there have been more than 20 million books sold on the topic. It is literally a household name for many people in business. With the wide use of any term, there is always misuse or misunderstanding, and guerrilla marketing is no different. Many people have mistakenly used the term to describe brand hijacking, pirate marketing, and underhanded business tactics like domain squatting or well-organized web attacks on websites.

Brand hijacking and pirate marketing are designing a website, picking a company name, or using corporate colors of other businesses in an attempt to confuse the customer and capitalize on someone else's hard branding work. Although this may be technically legal and difficult to dispute in a court of law, it is unethical and not part of the guerrilla way. Unethical actions are poisonous and once discovered will spread throughout your entire network, killing your credibility.

THREE DIRECTIONS AT ONCE

To hit your lofty business goals you need a business growth strategy that is geometric, not incremental in its growth. Your business growth needs to happen in three ways all at once. These three ways are 1) more profitable transactions, 2) more frequent transactions, and 3) referral transactions.

More Profitable Transactions

Profit is a function of awareness and obsession. It is the measuring stick that guerrillas use to keep focused. Traffic, sentiment, popularity, or desire for coolness only lead you down the wrong path. If you have to work 18 hours per day to turn a profit, you're actually broke. Time is money, and it's also what life is made of. Search constantly for ways to become more efficient in your business and marketing activities. True profit is having a financial net gain plus the time and the relationships to enjoy the bounty. Some areas to focus on to drive profit:

- *ROI on marketing activities.* Constantly evaluate and tweak the type of social media you use and how you use it. Always look for best practices and ways to improve and increase your results.
- *Efficiency in procurement and manufacturing.* Technology and social networks can help you reduce your cost of procurement and manufacturing significantly. Find ways to improve your distribution and payment terms with suppliers. Also look at ways to carry fewer inventories using just-in-time inventory systems and manufacturing partners.
- *Customer follow-up and retention.* Repeat customers are more profitable than new customers. Once established, customer relationships can be perpetuated with much less investment than it took to get them started. Too many salespeople, marketers, and business owners are too focused on new business. They miss the diamonds scattered in their own backyard. Make nurturing and growing existing customer relationships a priority. It's a very profitable act.

➤ *Outsourcing and delegating.* Question everything about your business processes. Are there expensive business processes that you can outsource and have done for less? Are there well-paid staff or executives doing things that should be delegated to more junior staff? Are there manual processes that can be automated? Find ways to get lean by outsourcing, automating, and delegating.

More Frequent Transactions

Velocity of cash flow is very important to business growth. Frequent purchases create that velocity. Frequent purchases come from ongoing value-added contact and because you always know what's next. Plan your marketing strategy to intentionally expand use of products and services by your customer. After an initial purchase are you sending additional offers via e-mail? Are you engaging existing customers online and monitoring their activity for potential signs that they have a need for what you offer? Do you look for additional products and services from fusion partners that you could offer to your clients? Start thinking about ways you can create more frequent purchases.

Referral Transactions

Generating business via referrals is another leveraged method of generating sales. Guerrillas have multiple ways for people to refer business to them. The most important factor is that you must be referable. To be referable is about keeping promises, supplying a superior product or service, and providing an incredible customer experience. All of these play a big role in how successful you will be generating referrals. You must also make it easy for people to refer business to you. Make sure all of your business information is easy to share and in multiple media formats online.

IT'S ABOUT THEM

Most corporate blogs and websites are dry and boring. Traditional marketers tend to create a lot of content about them. They are Me Marketers. Most marketing is also too sanitized and a monologue. Social media doesn't allow this to work. When someone hits your blog and it doesn't talk about them, their challenges, and what's important to their life, they leave and never come back. If you don't allow them to make comments on your site or post negative feedback, they will use tools like Google Sidewiki, Yelp, Twitter, or Facebook to tell the world how they feel. Today you can't sanitize your brand and no one wants a monologue. They want to be heard.

Instead of writing headlines, write engagement lines.

Guerrilla social media marketers get customer-focused by:

- ➤ Diving deep into online communities and answering and asking questions
- ➤ Writing web content that doesn't boast about corporate greatness but talks about solutions to the customers' challenges
- ➤ Listening, responding, and helping instead of using marketing monologues.
- ➤ Providing multiple channels for feedback through major social networks and tools like Live chat.

MASH UP

Guerrillas mash up media, networks, and ideas to collaboratively create powerful marketing campaigns. Too many people are us vs. them people. They tend to debate which media is best, contrasting print advertising vs. web advertising, Twitter vs. Facebook, or blogging vs.

YouTube channels. You need to understand that any of these tools alone will never be as effective as an integrated marketing strategy using multiple media and marketing activities. A mash up is a combination of multiple media, and those marketing combinations greatly increase the speed and effectiveness of your engagement strategy.

> Using more than one channel and social media tool shortens your brand engagement curve.

The Altimeter Group and Wetpaint did an in-depth study of the world's top 100 brands using social media. Their findings indicated that those brands that used multiple social media weapons and marketing combinations developed a significantly higher level of engagement online than those that only used a few social media tools.

Don't just stop at mashing up online media; take it a step further and ensure that you use traditional guerrilla marketing weapons to augment your social media attack. One of the things that makes Starbucks such a powerful social media brand is the fact that it has so much offline marketing, advertising, and brand exposure. Although we will be working on a seven-sentence social media marketing plan in this book, it's important that you as a guerrilla marketer have an overall marketing plan that complements and works with your social media plan.

UPSIDE-DOWN MARKETERS

Guerrillas make sure their social media activity is 90 percent connection and community contribution, and 10 percent well-placed and customized marketing messages. When people think of marketing, traditionally it's a well-crafted, sanitized, and polished message that is pushed out to the consumer. Social media is social. Much of your success will be based upon your ability to build social capital and trust with the community networks you're part of.

People are overwhelmed with noise. From television to radio to direct mail and even to Twitter, there's just too much chatter for the average consumer to focus. Some people argue that a well-written blog entry or a clever marketing piece can get above that noise and be the signal. The greatest beacon you can have in marketing that helps you permanently stand above the noise is relationships. When traditional marketers send out a tweet, a direct-mail piece, or an e-mail blast, the question is, "What can I get from these people?" The message is usually about why you should buy something from them and make them a profit.

The businesses that are profiting the most from social media purposefully and consistently look for ways to add value and deepen relationships with the online community. Sometimes adding value is as easy as simply listening to customers and letting them know they've been heard. Other times it may mean creating an entire community platform or social network that specifically talks to the needs and desires of your target market. When you're putting together your contribution strategy, think about ways that you can help and contribute that are unique. In addition to being unique, contribute more than your competitors think is practical and get more intimate than other marketers feel is comfortable.

TECHNOLOGY SAVVY

Technology is not a casual love affair for guerrilla social media marketers. You must be married to technology. This means mastering the social media weapons you use so that you can outperform and outengage any competitor on any playing field. By listening to your customers intently and watching their movements and behaviors online, you'll begin to develop the ability to spot trends and identify which tools you need to master. Ultimately, it's about your customers and your prospects, so don't worry about the latest, greatest, newest technology that other marketers are talking about.

Sometimes the technology your customers want to use isn't sexy. Using those platforms may not win you awards from your peers, but they will make you profits.

NANO-CASTERS

Guerrillas build an army of supporters and customers one very personal interaction at a time. Too many marketers spend too much time in their ivory towers and not enough time on the street where their customers are. Using nano-casting to reach your nano-markets gives you a key competitive advantage over others in the marketplace.

There are many ways to nano-cast, depending upon your business. A fitness club with ten locations in different cities can nano-cast by setting up individual Twitter accounts and blogs for each location. Each location will have its own demographic group with specific interests and lifestyle that is driven by region. You will find online that many organizations will have one corporate Twitter account and a corporate blog that talks generally to a broad audience. The most important audience for those fitness clubs is the people within two miles of that location. Local staff members writing local blog entries and having conversations with their community can more effectively engage and develop relationships than a faraway corporate voice. But that alone is not nano-casting; that's really niche-casting. A guerrilla would take her lists of Twitter folk in her region that she follows and create specific lists of people. They could be broken down by what fitness classes they attend, fitness level, gender, exercise preferences, and even nutrition interests. It would enable her to have very specific and personal conversations, establishing a deeper level of rapport than a generic marketing tweet or corporate reply.

Another example of nano-casting could be a YouTube auto care video series specifically for people who collect Chevy trucks produced between 1945 and 1960. The companies that would bene-fit from this series would be an aftermarket parts manufacturer, a metal fabricator, or a do-it-yourself auto magazine publisher. That one nano-market may not be enough to build a business on, but if you were to produce ten different series based upon various vehicle makes, those ten nano-markets could easily help you build a prof-itable business.

ATTENTION TO DETAIL

Mind-blowing customer experience is what sets guerrilla mar-keters above the rest. Today, although customers are more con-nected than ever, their expectations for major corporations around service are actually quite low. Major corporations and tra-ditional marketers take advantage of this and deliver acceptable, mediocre service.

The magic in delivering a mind-blowing customer experience is its ability to turn customers into raving fans and raving fans into advocates. With all the social media at their fingertips, your cus-tomers have now taken ownership of your brand and through their conversations with you and others can lift that brand up or tear it to shreds.

Paying attention to detail in social media means paying atten-tion to how quickly your blog loads, how efficiently you respond, the implied tone in your tweets, and how user-friendly your contact form is on your website. Attention to detail also means using social media to monitor specific customers and understand everything about them, from what restaurants they like to where they go on holiday, to what their favorite sports team is. Use this detailed infor-mation to deliver customized, specific customer experiences to peo-ple. When your customers discover you have taken the time to learn more about them, you're no longer a pitch artist and marketer; you're a trusted advisor and friend.

HONOR RELATIONSHIPS AND VALUE PERMISSION

Conventional business wisdom spawned the saying, "It's not personal, it's just business." Guerrillas know customers take the way you treat them very personally. At the end of a marketing campaign, most people count the number of tweets, website visits, Facebook friends, and YouTube video views that they amassed during the campaign. At the end of your marketing campaign, you need to focus on how many new relationships you started and how many existing relationships you deepened to greater levels of consent. Although profit is how we need to measure the success of our marketing over time, strong customer relationships are what lead to those profits.

> Permission to connect has put the power in the consumer's hands. Seek and then treat that permission like gold.

Relationships lead to a point where the customer will give you consent to market specific things of interest to them. As Jay Levinson says, "Never fail to distinguish between your B List customers who should be treated like royalty, and your A List customers, who should be treated like family."

There are several levels of relationship development in social media. In fact after the initial purchase by a customer, most marketers and salespeople feel their job is done. The initial purchase is actually just the beginning of a long-term profitable relationship based upon genuinely contributing and connecting at all stages. Before the purchase there are several stages of relationship development that you will move through with customers: the five stages of consent.

> It's kind of like dating. Don't ask someone to marry you on the first date.

The five stages of consent are:

1. Discovery
2. Consumption
3. Interaction
4. Connection
5. Consent

Discovery

Discovery is exactly what it sounds like. For the marketer, you will discover new clients and new community members through the use of guerrilla intelligence tools and, of course, referrals from the community. For consumers, discovery can happen in many ways. They may hear your name tweeted several times by their community, their friend may e-mail them a link to an interesting blog article you've written, or Google can deliver them right to your website through a keyword search. This step is about finding the right connections and being found by the right connections. One of the reasons why guerrillas always have to be on and ready to engage is that we usually have less than 15 seconds to make that good first impression to move consumers to the next step. We cover this in greater depth when we talk about building your guerrilla headquarters, which is your blog or social site. It is, however, vital that your website or blog is designed in a way that immediately establishes credibility with the audience you are targeting.

Consumption

Now that you've qualified to qualify and the visitors have not abandoned your site or clicked away from your Twitter profile, they will begin to consume the content you create. Too many people at this point immediately spring into action, blasting their visitors or new connections with marketing messages, special offers, and various other types of Me Marketing.

In order to engage, establish trust, and make people want to invest more time, energy, and effort into learning about us and what we can do for them, guerrillas need to exceed their expectations with high-value content. This is where the quality of your blog writing, the helpfulness of your studies and white papers, and the entertainment value of your YouTube videos all become very important. You gain consent by being trustworthy, and trust is based upon credibility. Credibility is challenging because it is contextual. Every human being has a slightly different definition or set of values that drives what they feel is valuable. Some people who read two blog posts they like about you may sign up for your e-mail newsletter and send you a quick tweet. Other people may read your blog for six months, follow your Twitter stream, and lurk about on Facebook observing you before you ever know they're there. Consistently produced high-value content using multiple social media weapons ensures that your visitors can consume the information they want in the format they want it in at a time that is right for them. All of this leads to interaction, where the customer you don't know hits your radar.

Interaction

Interaction can happen in several ways. Sometimes you can jump right to the interaction stage if the timing is right. If you own an automotive garage and notice that someone on Twitter asked a question about winter tires, it is most likely this person would be open to you interacting with him and giving him answers. Interaction can also occur by your being proactive and visiting the blogs, Twitter profiles, and Facebook pages of your target market and making value-added comments and initiating conversations. The other form of interaction is, of course, the customer-driven version where, after reading your blog for a time, prospects begin making comments. They may even ask a question or contribute their own content to your Facebook page or Flickr group, or share a tweet of yours with their followers. All of these are door openers to the next stage of relationship development.

Connection

Connection is a soft step in the stages of consent but is often mistaken for consent to market. Connection is when someone adds you as a friend on Facebook, a connection on LinkedIn, or mutually follows you on Twitter. In the world of dating, it would be the equivalent of a connection on Match.com; it doesn't mean you're going to agree to go on a date, but it does say I'd like to learn more about you. It also says I would like you to learn a little bit more about me. Resist the temptation to push marketing messages, special offers, and all those other types of Me Marketing at your connections. At this point the person wants to learn more about you, not buy from you. This step is very important credibility building. When someone connects with you on Facebook or LinkedIn, in particular, that person is allowing us to see more of his world, his business, and his personality, and to adjust our marketing and communications to match his credibility model and values.

Consent

If relationships were currency, consent would be the gold standard. A lot of companies spend a lot of time gaining customers but neglect to truly build relationships, and so they miss long-term opportunities. On the other hand, there are a lot of social media marketers who have friendly chats, feel very liked and popular, but lack consent to market. Consent is where you move from feel-good, fuzzy marketing to monetization. You have consent when someone has agreed to subscribe to your newsletter and has given you an e-mail address for that purpose. Consent can also be in the form of a question or inquiry over Twitter, when someone asks you a specific question about a service you offer or a product you sell. Other forms of consent are when someone attends a free webinar by your company. It is usually assumed that you will give real educational value, but also at the end of your webinar people expect a certain level of marketing or information on your product or services. After your webinar, a follow-up e-mail thanking people for attending and providing some information on your business and offerings is also acceptable. Offline connections where someone bumps into you at an event and lets you know he wants to learn more about your business is, of course, one of the oldest forms of consent. Guerrillas value this level of permission so much that they are very careful to respect boundaries and still keep a good ratio of high-value content interaction relative to marketing-speak or offers.

> When I join your Facebook page, give you my e-mail, or follow you on Twitter, those are examples of "permission to connect."

A proper guerrilla marketing attack has a beginning, a middle, but in most cases, no end. The same holds true for relationships. Once consent is gained, you move through your natural sales or marketing process with that prospect. During this period, customers will still be consuming your great content on your blogs, Twitter, Google Buzz, or any other platform they're connected to you on. The difference is these tools now are used to expand the customer's knowledge of what you can do for them and expand your knowledge of their core needs, challenges, and goals.

After the initial sale, your goal is to continue to develop greater levels of intimacy, insight, and relationship with your customers. It costs a lot of money to gain a good, loyal customer, and guerrillas use relationships as insurance on that investment. If nurtured properly, those relationships can pay year after year in the form of direct purchases as well as referrals.

Guerrilla social media marketing is both a strategy and a way of thinking and living virtual lives. It's about applying time-tested principles of community-building, relationship development, innovation, and imagination to the lightning-fast world of digital social networks. As we have said earlier, a guerrilla social media marketing attack has a beginning, a middle, but no end. You need to sustain that attack for one year or even longer before you reap the full benefits. Guerrillas know that in order to sustain a vibrant and powerful marketing campaign, they must have a home base from which to launch. In the next chapter you learn how to build and protect your guerrilla social media marketing headquarters.

CHAPTER 8

BUILDING AND PROTECTING YOUR GUERRILLA HQ

Every guerrilla needs a headquarters. In the past that would have been an office, retail store, or any other type of business location. It's a place from which to launch your guerrilla marketing efforts and it's also a place to drive customers and business to. Your headquarters is where you convert curious visitors to loyal customers and advocates. Today your guerrilla social media headquaters is a blog or social site. It's is vital that you build a solid foundation from which all of your social media efforts will

originate. It's also a place for community to form and communicate with
you and each other.

In the following pages we will talk
about key areas that you need to focus
on to have an effective blog or socialized
website. Before we get into these ten key
areas here is a brief summary of what
you will learn about:

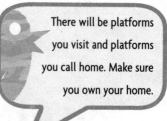

There will be platforms
you visit and platforms
you call home. Make sure
you own your home.

1. *Social sites versus traditional websites.* Social sites are growing
   constantly through content created and generated by visitors,
   clients, and partners. Guerrillas must understand the difference between a traditional website and a social site, then they
   must ensure that their headquarters (blog or site) is very
   social and engaging.

2. *Engagement pages versus landing pages.* Engagement pages are
   designed to capture hearts and minds not just e-mail
   addresses. Guerrillas know that customers want options not
   ultamatums and build web pages that allow the customer to
   drive the learning and buying process.

3. *Subscription options.* Guerrillas provide multiple methods
   and mediums to subscribe to all in one place including
   video, RSS, iTunes, and newsletter subscriptions. This is
   important because not everyone learns or researches the
   same way. Multiple options means maximum conversion
   opportunities.

4. *Socialized and networked.* All of the guerrillas networks are
   accessible from one place. This makes is easy for people to
   connect with you on multiple networks. Redundancy is key.
   Aggregating offsite content about you is also vital. By
   pulling in all of the conversations and content created by
   you and about your business you will have a constant stream
   of fresh content that your visitors can easily access.

5. *Keep it simple.* Guerrillas use well known inexpensive and easy-to-deploy blogging and social website tools. They don't get bogged down in excessively expensive and complex tools.

6. *Keep it focused.* The guerrilla home base is easy to navigate and use. It's also free of anything that does not appeal to his target market or contribute to his long-term goal. Most marketing fails because it is too general or it's unfocused and uncoordinated. Guerrilla bloggers understand their most profitable nano-markets and keep their blog or social site focused on serving those markets.

7. *Automate.* Technology is used to speed up mundane and repetitive tasks so that the guerrilla social media marketer can spend more time interacting with the community. You need to constantly automate tasks that are repetitive, mundane, or not focused on building profits or community.

8. *Analyze.* Site and network analytics tools are vital. What gets measured gets improved. The guerrilla social media marketer uses technology to measure everything on and off the home base. Sound analaytics tools allows you to do everything from proving ROI to learning more about your customer. Without analytics you will never know which marketing investments are effective and which ones are losing you time and money.

9. *Aggregated content for everyone.* Some people like lengthy white papers, others learn best through video, audio, or bite-sized text updates. Some content will be created by you, and other content will be pulled from people and places on the web. Guerrillas build all of these into their site and blog. Your website or blog must truly use multiple social media if you are to maximize engagement and visitor retention.

10. *Google love.* The guerrilla makes it easy to find his site by being a guerrilla search engine optimizer. Google still drives more traffic to websites than any other website, social media site, or social network. Many of your Twitter followers, blog

subscribers, or YouTube viewers will find you by searching on a certain topic in Google. You must get good at dominating the Google search results for keywords that bring you new visitors, subscribers, and business.

We are now going to take a look at each of the points in-depth.

SOCIAL SITES VS. TRADITIONAL WEBSITES

It is vital that your website be well socialized. Your visitors need and expect multiple options to communicate with you and each other.

If people land on your site or blog and it's not interactive, current, and engaging, they will often leave immediately never to return. Making sure that your site or blog is social will ensure that people will stick around to learn more about your company, products, services, and organizational values. As a reference we have created an at-a-glance comparison between traditional websites and social sites. When looking at your own blog or site make sure you meet all of the characteristics of a social site. See Figure 8.1 for a comparison of social sites vs. traditional websites.

FIGURE 8.1

Social Sites vs. Traditional Websites

Social Sites	Traditional Sites
Require very little knowledge to update and almost anyone can add content	Require technical knowledge to update and add content
Written for the customer about things that can help him	Full of me-focused marketing and are written like a corporate brochure

FIGURE 8.1

Social Sites vs. Traditional Websites, continued

Social Sites	Traditional Sites
Allow for bidirectional communication between guerrillas and their visitors, and also allow visitors to share and communicate with one another	Are unidirectional in their mode of communication
Are community hubs; push content out to guerrilla outposts and also pull in and aggregate content from those networks	Is a marketing island
Are easy to keep on the top of search engine rankings because of constantly added content by guerrillas and their visitors	Are difficult to keep on the top of search engine rankings because of their static nature
Make all of their content easy to share and repurpose	Lock up and protect their content, such as videos
Are full of value-added content, tools, and information that benefit their market, and don't require you to give consent before adding value	Require visitors' contact details and consent before establishing a relationship or providing any real value-added content
Due to their open source nature, are inexpensive or free to upgrade. This also allows for inexpensive redesigns	Require expensive custom plug-ins or web-based applications and a significant financial investment when upgrading the look and feel
Typically community-supported	Typically corporate-supported
Provides multiple methods for connecting with your company and provides access to multiple people within your organization	Provides limited channels and access to limited number of people within a company

Remember: Making sure that your site is fully socialized is a key ingredient in making sure that the traffic that arrives at your website stays and engages vs. quickly bouncing off.

ENGAGEMENT PAGES VS. LANDING PAGES

Engagement pages are designed to capture hearts and minds, not just e-mail addresses. Traditional internet marketers, on the other hand, rely heavily on controlling the behavior of their visitors. This means reducing options and choices. What is commonly referred to as a squeeze page is a good example of this. Squeeze pages usually are completely void of navigation buttons or links to other pages or websites. They give the visitor one of two choices: to read the marketing copy and then make a choice to either fill in personal information and give consent or to leave. Although this will capture a percentage of visitors who are ready, willing, or able to buy or give consent right now, it also repels visitors who could have become good clients if they had only been engaged in a credible manner.

Engagement pages have some similarities with a squeeze page in that their purpose is also to gain consent and generate subscribers. The difference is that the engagement page offers the visitor multiple options, mediums, and pathways to learn more about how the guerrilla's business can benefit and add value to the visitor's life or business. It also provides multiple subscription options.

SUBSCRIPTION OPTIONS

Guerrillas provide visitors multiple methods and mediums to connect with their business, including video, RSS, iTunes, and newsletter subscriptions, all in one place. There are several advantages to doing this:

- → Different people absorb information in different manners. Some prefer to learn by watching videos; others only want bite-sized pieces of information through tools like Twitter; and many want more in-depth information through subscribing to your blog and newsletters.

➤ By consuming multiple social media created by you, consumers' engagement level increases more and faster than if they only get their information from one type of social media. Being able to watch some videos, listen to a podcast, read a blog entry, and follow a few tweets increases frequency of exposure.

➤ It creates redundancy in your connections so that if your customers stop using a specific social network or decide to no longer read your newsletter, you still have multiple points of contact with them.

SOCIALIZED AND NETWORKED

All of the guerrilla's networks are accessible from one place. This makes it easy for people to connect with you on multiple networks. Redundancy is key. Aggregating off-site content about you is also vital.

What Does It Mean to Be Socialized?

Being socialized means every page on a site is very easy to share and promote to the visitor's network. It also means that the network provides multiple methods for bidirectional communication. WordPress plug-ins like ShareThis, TweetThis, or BuzzIt give the visitor the ability to share what he's reading with dozens of different social networks of which he's a member. Don't make your visitors work hard to promote you. They shouldn't have to cut and paste the URL of the page they're reading, drop it into a URL shrinker, and write a juicy headline to share it with their community. Only a small portion of visitors will work this hard for you. Many people will share your content if all it takes is one click to share it to Facebook, Twitter, or their Google Buzz profile.

Clearly List Your Networks

Prominently display links to all the social network profiles that you and your company are using, including links to your Twitter profile, Facebook pages or profiles, other blogs you have, LinkedIn profiles and groups, your YouTube channel, and any other guerrilla social media outpost that you are actively engaging on. Earlier we mentioned that guerrilla social media outposts help drive traffic to your social site; your social site, in turn, helps connect people to your social profiles. Your headquarters and your outposts feed each other and perpetuate growth in both areas.

AGGREGATED CONTENT FOR EVERYONE

Much of the conversation by the community about your brand happens off-site and at outposts. Guerrillas pull those conversations and aggregate them on their sites. With a little help from your WordPress developer or your CMS provider, you can pull conversations from Twitter, photos from Flickr, videos from YouTube, and content from other social networks all into one place on your site. Your visitors can then get a complete picture of the crowd's feeling about your brand. A list of client testimonials posted on your site is great, but providing access to actual people who are talking about your brand right now has far greater impact. Where a wall of client testimonials only shows a sanitized view of your brand, being willing to share all the conversations about your brand shows a high level of confidence and transparency.

> Pull all of the conversations about your brand into one place. Make it easy for your customers and prospects to learn about you.

By aggregating these fragmented conversations about your brand into one place, it reduces the amount of work potential customers have to do to research you. Once again, the easier you make it for people to learn about you and share their thoughts about your brand, the higher your response rates will be.

KEEP IT SIMPLE

Guerrillas use well-known, inexpensive, and easy-to-deploy blogging and social website tools. They don't get bogged down in excessively expensive and complex tools. The most important thing in your social media marketing is your message and your conversations. This is not a complex concept requiring really complex tools. The more elaborate your technology and the more difficult it is to use, the less time you're going to spend on crafting your message and having valuable conversations. Most social media tools are designed to be user friendly. Avoid the ones that aren't. The only thing complex or difficult to use tools to do is create a barrier to entry for many people on your team. If it's not easy, in most cases people find it difficult to form the habit of consistently using them.

Don't fall in love with fancy social media tools, fall in love with your customer instead.

KEEP IT FOCUSED

The guerrilla home base is easy to navigate and use, it's also free of anything that does not appeal to its target market or contribute to its long-term goal. Your website navigation should be designed intuitively. Don't get too creative. Stick to a format that 99 percent of all blogs and websites use. Your visitors will be able to quickly find what they're looking for this way and not have to fumble around to find it. That way your website's designed reflects how easy it is to do business with you.

Your site should be designed with the singular focus of gaining consent, which will drive profits. Be wary of any site design that includes gratuitous use of graphic design elements such as Flash splash pages or very large graphic headers that take up prime real estate on your website. A beautiful header and a flash intro may make your visitor say, "Wow, that's cool," but it's not going to motivate her to give you consent to market. Really large headers take a long time to load, if they load at all. The other factor is that many people now spend a lot of time browsing the internet using mobile devices and very few mobile browsers can view Flash at all. Big images take up the entire screen, burying all of your valuable social content and the navigation buttons.

AUTOMATE

Technology is used to speed up mundane and repetitive tasks so that the guerrilla social media marketer can spend more time interacting with the community. Automate everything other than intimacy-generating conversations. Instead of cutting and pasting comments about your brand and putting them in a blog post, for example, use a tool like Yahoo Pipes to automatically pull in multiple streams of information and republish them on your site without ever having to cut and paste a single thing.

> Automate mundane and left brain type activity. This will free you up to do more creative and innovative guerrilla marketing.

With tools like Hootsuite you can pull your blog feed into Twitter and each time you update your blog it automatically tweets it for you. You can also pre-schedule blog posts; this allows you to blog in your downtime or non-productive hours and not stop in the middle of your day to post your entry. It also allows you to publish your posts at the point in the day when they will generate the most traffic, regardless of your own engagement at that hour. As you already know, there are dozens of guerrilla social media weapons that you can use to automate multiple processes and activities on your website and in your business.

ANALYZE

Site and network analytics tools are vital. What gets measured gets improved. The guerrilla social media marketer uses technology to measure everything on and off your home base. A lot of people advise you just to create good content and great conversations, and not obsess over statistics. We've all heard the analogy that you can't make a goal with your eyes on the scoreboard. While you shouldn't obsess over statistics, you should learn from them. Social media and social networks move so fast that you can't afford to check your statistics just once in awhile. Tuning into your website analytics as well as your social media monitoring tools several times a day helps you measure and adjust your marketing message. It is important if you have a sudden spike in traffic and visitors to know about it immediately so you can fully capitalize on that spike while it's happening. If people are tweeting links to your blog and saying great things (or horrible things) you need to be able to connect with them immediately to thank them for their feedback or address their concerns.

"What gets inspected gets respected, and what gets measured can improve."
Captain Trevor Greene, "Peace Warrior"

GOOGLE LOVE

Guerrillas make it easy to find their site by being a guerrilla search engine optimizer. Blogging alone will not increase website traffic and not every potential customer will be active on social networks. Almost everyone on the planet who's looking for something will first search Google, Bing, or Yahoo for it. When we talk about Google

Love, what we're really talking about is making sure your website is structured and your content is written in a way that gives you high rankings for key search terms that your target market would use to find you.

Here are some quick tips on getting Google Love:

> Having a great search engine marketing strategy ensures that you can grow your community and list quickly. Remember, the first step in gaining consent is being discovered.

→ Don't use a website software that spawns pages from a database that produces long strings of code that communicate nothing to Google about what your site is about. Your blogging or site software must produce permalinks that are named and describe what your blog entry or page is about. An example of a page with a long string of nondescriptive code would be something such as http://yoursite.com/?=page1436.php. You want the pages to be spawned using a descriptive permalink such as http://yoursite.com/how-to-lose-weight.

→ With your blog, make sure that you use tags and categories for each post. Tags are short, descriptive terms or single words that describe what the blog post is about. Categories, of course, indicate the overreaching topic that the blog entry is about. Search engines take this into account when determining the relevance of your blog site to a search.

→ Take the time to put specific and custom metadata into each page that you write. Metadata is code that's not visible to the human eye but tells search engine crawlers what the page is about. The most important metadata is the page title. Choose your page title wisely. It should include words and terms that people looking for your type of solutions or products would punch into a search engine.

➤ Keyword-rich blog entries and pages will help drive your search engine rankings up. Don't overuse keywords, but in a 200-word blog entry or page, you should mention your major keywords four to five times each. Overdoing it could cause Google or other search engines to punish you for keyword stuffing.

➤ Use media-like pictures in your posts. Google and Bing both have comprehensive image search functionality. When you upload a photo to your website, you can add a description of what the photo is about that is hidden to the human eye but visible to search engines. You can also add captions and carefully choose the name of the image to be optimized for keywords that people may search for. Taking the time to do this will help increase search engine traffic.

➤ Use all the guerrilla social media weapons that enhance your search engine visibility. This would include Google sitemaps, and if you're using WordPress as your website or blogging software, plug-ins like AllInOneSEO and PushPress can greatly help search engines find you.

➤ Avoid using duplicate content across the web. If Google identifies that you've taken the same blog entry and posted it on multiple sites in your network in an attempt to game the system, they may knock one or all of your websites and social profiles off of the Google index. Being booted off Google is basically internet bankruptcy.

The ten key areas of focus for creating a successful guerrilla social media headquarters are vital. We have taken the key characterisitics and attributes of an effective social site that we discussed and put them into a checklist for you (Figure 8.2). You can use this checklist to review your existing site and see what needs to be improved or added. You can also use this checklist to help you do an intitial blog or site design spec for your next website or blog.

FIGURE 8.2
Your Social Site Checklist

When you upgrade your website to be social or when you want to build a completely new site, give this list to your developer to ensure that your new site is completely socialized and guerrillified.

- ❏ Has built-in e-mail list-building technology such as AWeber or Constant Contact forms
- ❏ Requires very little technical knowledge to update so that almost anyone can add content
- ❏ Text is written for the customer about things that can help the customer
- ❏ Allows for bidirectional communications and conversations on-site
- ❏ Makes all of the content on the website easy to share and repurpose using social bookmarking and sharing technology
- ❏ Is open source, giving you access to a large pool of inexpensive developers and upgrades
- ❏ Gives visitors multiple options for communicating with your organization
- ❏ Includes engagement pages that offer multiple options for learning about your business
- ❏ Includes multiple subscription options including RSS feeds, video feeds, newsletter subscriptions, and more
- ❏ Is totally socialized, and does not make your visitors work hard to promote you
- ❏ Promptly displays links to all the social profiles that you and your company are using
- ❏ Aggregates and pulls relevant conversations from Twitter, photos from Flickr, videos from YouTube, and content from other social networks onto your site

FIGURE 8.2
Your Social Site Checklist, continued

❑ Is easy to navigate and has a built-in function for searching the entire site by keyword

❑ Is mobile-device-friendly and easy to view

❑ Does not include gratuitous use of graphic design elements such as Flash pages or really large headers that take up valuable space

❑ Automates some of your social media activities, including posting links to your latest blog entry to Twitter and the capacity to preschedule blog posts

❑ Has comprehensive measurement and analytics tools built into the site

❑ Is integrated with social media monitoring tools to track your level of net engagement on a daily basis

❑ Uses descriptive permalinks

❑ Gives you the ability to tag pages and blog entries, and also categorize them

❑ Enables the user to easily add metadata to pages without any web or programming knowledge

❑ Has Google sitemaps and SEO plug-ins

Once you have your guerrilla headquarters established and fully socialized, you will then be ready to begin launching your guerrilla social media marketing attack and start recruiting and partnering with other guerrillas.

CHAPTER 9

RECRUITING AND PARTNERING WITH GUERRILLAS

 The only way to truly scale social media efforts is to leverage other people's networks and communities. Your goal as a guerrilla social media marketer is not to just build your own online communities. Your goal is to tap into the networks of other guerrillas and get them to help pass your message on and expand your reach.

You need to build your own loyal following and community. This takes time, hard work, imagination, and innovation. The growth of your community may not be at a pace that supports your goals, and establishing trust and credibility is not something you can usually rush. By tapping into the networks of credible influencers and other guerrillas, you can accelerate your business growth. An endorsement from another guerrilla leader can help move you through several levels of consent. The right introduction and testimonial can move you from discovery to connection and then consent in a very short time.

> Seeing someone as a competitor is old economy. Seeing them as a peer and a fusion partner is key.

Partnerships and endorsements are also risky. The credibility of your personal brand and company are at stake with any partnership. Just because someone has a big e-mail list or Facebook page following doesn't necessarily make him a great partner. No, not even if that list is full of people or companies that match your targeting criteria. Your fusion partner must have values, ethics, attitudes, and attributes that are compatible with yours. Without that compatibility it will be a short-lived romance that could end up doing damage to your brand and asset base.

> When you're reaching out to thought leaders in the social space, you need to tap into their motivations.

In the following pages we will walk you through several vital topics that you need to master and understand when developing fusion parntnerships and garnering the support of other guerrillas. These vital topics include:

- → How to evaluate potential partners
- → Fusion partnerships
- → Methods of tapping into other guerrilla networks
- → How to become a network hub

EVALUATING PARTNERS

Some people rely on gut instinct to evaluate potential partners; others use a balance sheet approach, weighing the pros and cons of the potential relationship. Balance sheets can change, and gut instinct can be impacted by ego, fear, pride, and greed. Personal values are the foundation of any guerrilla enterprise.

Guerrillas identify their core values and build a career or life path that helps them live in congruence with these goals. This can have a massive effect on their productivity, health, energy, and happiness. Also, during stressful times, focusing on the goal and what you value can boost your energy and ability to handle temporary setbacks and obstacles. Knowing your values can also help you avoid short-term decisions in partnerships that can have long-term negative effects.

> When you come to a fork in the road and want to know what direction to take, understanding your core values will enable you to make the right choice for you.

Guerrillas define what success means to them and then build a business and network that helps them achieve that success. How you define success is driven by your own values, not by how society or your peers define it. Too many people only pursue lofty financial goals or fame because of external forces. Those same people arrive at their goal tired, off purpose, and still unsatisfied. It is a big challenge, but we want you to identify your values and build everything else around that, including your fusion partnerships.

Fred Shadian is a long term mentor of Shane Gibson. He is an author, professional speaker, and acclaimed martial artist. Fred teaches an invaluable values exploration exercise that we now use regularly at out guerrilla social media marketing seminars. He calls it "values mapping." It provides a wider variety of flexibility than most formal or structured values mapping tools, but it takes only 15 to 60 minutes to identify your top five to seven values.

The process is straightforward. First you list seven things that you would absolutely love to do, achieve, or buy in your lifetime. Then take each goal and ask a simple question "Why is that important to you?" Often the answer is somewhat superficial at first, but as you continue to dig deeper, you identify the core value or motivator that drives the goal. What is interesting is that once you identify your values, you often find that there are many goals and options that satisfy those values.

After you identify your top five to seven goals you would take each goal individually and identify the core value that drives the need to achieve that goal. You would do this with each of the goals separately in order to identify your core values. Figure 9.1 is a diagram of how you would walk through this values exploration exercise with one goal. (This would then be repeated five to seven times with different goals in order to identify multiple values.)

Once you have completed this exercise with all seven goals, prioritize them from most important to least important as in Figure 9.2. This helps set meaningful goals in all areas of your life, and it is extremely helpful in helping you engage in activities and relationships that are congruent with your core goals.

Although potential partners may not have mapped their goals as you have, you can identify their values by asking questions, observing choices they make, and listening to their interactions with others. Even how someone treats a server in a restaurant or how they respond to a random question on Twitter can say a lot.

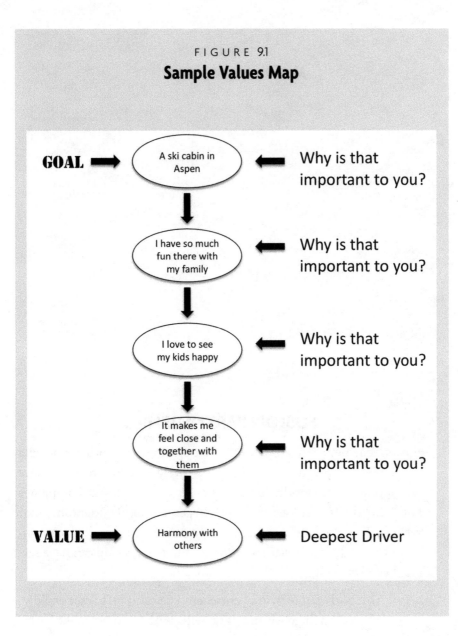

FIGURE 9.1

Sample Values Map

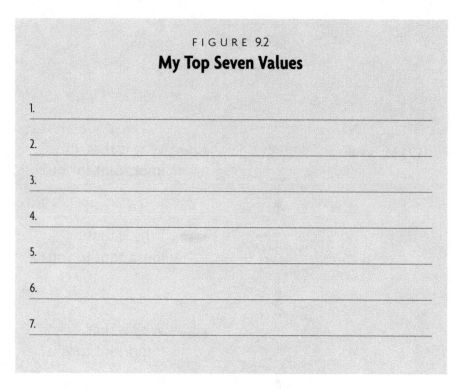

FIGURE 9.2
My Top Seven Values

1. _____

2. _____

3. _____

4. _____

5. _____

6. _____

7. _____

FUSION PARTNERSHIPS

Fusion partnerships are about collaborating with other guerrilla marketers and businesses online. The core goal is to cross-promote and leverage one another's marketing efforts. Seek out companies and individuals that have the same target market demographic that you do. These people should have a noncompeting or even complimentary product or service to offer. A solid partnership can have several benefits:

- ➤ You both can increase your client base and influence rapidly
- ➤ Shared intelligence and data helps both partners make better business decisions
- ➤ Reduced costs because marketing investments can be shared

➤ Collaborative value-added services and products because you can combine solutions to create a unique offering

➤ Safety in numbers; the more of the RIGHT partners you have, the larger your leveraged influence becomes

➤ Support and peer mentoring

In addition to seeking out those that have the same target markets as you, think about transference of technology and skills. Are there other applications for your technology, product, or service in industries you have not focused on? Does someone else possess a technology, product, or service that could be adapted and introduced to your client base? Remember that creativity, imagination, and innovation are a guerrilla's core competitive advantage. Apply those attributes to your fusion partner search.

TAPPING INTO OTHER GUERRILLA NETWORKS

There are many powerful influencers and leaders in almost every niche one can imagine online. Being able to target these leaders and have them spread your message is a key viral marketing strategy. To find fusion partners:

➤ Join networks, sites, and groups that your customers and prospects are part of. Seek out other marketers and community members who have much influence within those groups and communities.

➤ Ask your customers about who their suppliers are. Who delivers exceptional service and inspires customer loyalty within your target market?

➤ Look for online communities, membership sites, and events (online or offline) that have been created by another marketer who caters to your audience.

➤ Search for terms in Google that your prospects would search for, and make a note of who is buying targeted keyword advertising for that search. Reach out to those marketers that you feel would resonate with your values and business goals.

➤ Look for speakers, authors, trainers, analysts, bloggers and influential social networkers who are a source of inspiration and information for your target market. Drill down to the nano-market if possible.

CREATING SOCIAL EQUITY

Communities are like a high-interest-paying bank. The more you put into them, the higher your return on investment. Guerrilla marketers are big contributors; this contribution makes them trustworthy, credible, and referable. Social currency or capital gives you credibility and access to other community leaders and influencers.

> Best short-cut for results: focus on people, relationships, and psychology, not gimmicks and clicks.

Reciprocity

Rewarding someone for sending you a lead can be a great way to stimulate business. An even more effective way to generate genuine referrals and friends is to give first and give often to the people and communities that you want to be connected to. When you give something of real value without strings attached, people want to help you and promote your vision. It's a true gesture of genuine partnership and community involvement. This is really an exercise in awareness. Ask some of these questions to create awareness:

> Make a list of people who support you online. Develop a strategy to reciprocate.

➤ What goals do other guerrillas that you want to partner with have? How can you support them in attaining those goals?

➤ What do you have that costs you very little but has a high value with your target market?

➤ What unique information or insight can you contribute to the community?

➤ Who could you connect with someone else that would greatly benefit from the connection?

Ask these questions continually and take action when you see the opportunity to add value and build social capital.

Further ideas for building social capital with other leaders are:

➤ Do free podcasts that solve problems and help your collective target audience.

➤ Pick a guerrilla each week to meet in person or via direct communication such as Skype or Google Chat.

➤ Invite potential fusion partners into your network as a guest speaker for an event or webinar.

➤ Promote and profile other guerrillas on your blog, podcast, or video channel.

➤ Sponsor a community event.

➤ Get involved in a charity or fundraiser that potential partners are supporting.

➤ Put their blogs on your blogroll.

➤ Send leads and business opportunities their way.

➤ Give them the inside scoop on business trends, new technology, or anything that is valuable guerrilla intelligence.

Treat People Intelligently

There's an old marketing saying based upon the acronym KISS. It stands for "keep it simple stupid," and it implies that we must keep our marketing simple and idiot-proof. Why? Because old-school marketers think the marketplace is simple-minded and easy to confuse. But people aren't stupid and simple, especially other guerrillas that are potential fusion partners. These people are as smart as your mother; she knows what you're about to do even before you do.

Don't insult potential partners with insincere community contribution; they will see and feel your intent. To build social capital and an environment of partnership and reciprocity takes a genuine heart. Your mother can read you in a heartbeat and so can other guerrilla leaders and community members.

Figure 9.3 provides a checklist that helps you rate yourself, your potential fusion partner, and the partnership you are considering.

FIGURE 9.3

My Fusion Partnership Checklist

I have invested the time to know my top seven values, which are:

1. _____

2. _____

3. _____

4. _____

5. _____

6. _____

7. _____

I understand my target market and nano-markets: ❏ Yes ❏ No

I have built a considerable network of the people in my target market and have relationships and credibility down to the nano-market level: ❏ Yes ❏ No

---

FIGURE 9.3

My Fusion Partnership Checklist, continued

I have established myself as a network hub and have built considerable social capital; this will give me significant social capital and leverage in developing my partnership:

❏ Yes ❏ No

I have spent time researching my potential fusion partner and understand their values and goals:

❏ Yes ❏ No

My potential fusion partner's target market is the same as mine or has a strong potential as a potential user of my products or services

❏ Yes ❏ No

My potential fusion partner's values and goals complement or are congruent with my values and goals:

❏ Yes ❏ No

My potential fusion partner has the same or greater level of influence and social capital that I possess:

❏ Yes ❏ No

The services and products that we are jointly marketing are of mutually high value to our networks:

❏ Yes ❏ No

This fusion partnership has both short term and long term benefits for both parties:

❏ Yes ❏ No

The more brutally honest you can be in this process, the more time, money, energy, and reputation you can save yourself.

BE A NETWORK HUB

Guerrilla social media marketers are more than one node in a network; they are the hubs of many networks. The bigger your online community and the greater your influence, the more you have to offer fusion partners. A fusion partnership is always win/win. As you increase what you can bring to a partnership, you will attract and retain increasingly better partners. The following pages discuss ways to be a valued resource, community builder, and connector. Not all of these ideas will be applicable to everyone, but take note of the ideas you could use to become a network hub.

Network hubs are community builders: Your influence is a currency, which you use to trade with other guerrilla leaders. Influence is also a bargaining chip that you can use to shape a profitable deal. Building networks and communities and being connected to the right communities impacts your level of influence.

In building communities there are several angles of attack:

1. Build your own from scratch
2. Join a youthful or new network and grow with it
3. Tap into an existing network and establish a high profile

Build Your Own Community from Scratch

Scott Heiferman, CEO of Meetup.com, started Meetup to help communities self-organize around specific interests or community movements. Tools like Meetup, Ning, Facebook Pages and Facebook Groups, as well as white label social networking software, can be used to start your own online community. Look at your target market and community, then drill down to the nano-markets within them. What specific interests and hobbies do these people share? Is there a social network online or a Meetup group that you could start that would fill a void and elevate you to the level of community builder?

There are a number of things to consider in establishing your own community—both positive and negative. So carefully analyze the benefits before you start.

Advantages

➤ You establish the culture, tone, and format of events or the online interaction.

- ➤ The community can be designed and customized to reflect your branding.
- ➤ Offline events can have a level of marketing and advertising determined by you.
- ➤ When you introduce new members, they become part of your list of contacts.
- ➤ The community and network could later be sold as an asset to another entrepreneur.
- ➤ You have unfettered access to business intelligence generated by your community's actions, preferences, and feedback.
- ➤ Any referrals or opportunities flow directly to you.

Disadvantages

- ➤ It takes 6 to 18 months of consistent effort to gain momentum within a new network.
- ➤ There is an upfront investment needed in both time and money.
- ➤ You carry the burden of the ongoing costs until your network is large enough and engaged enough to generate revenue.
- ➤ On top of growing the network, as a founder you need to be a referee, moderator, and curator. These duties are both political and administrative in nature.

Building your own community network really isn't optional. It's something you need to do eventually. It advisable that you begin to build one, let it run its natural course, and employ one or all of the other strategies for becoming a network hub.

Grow with a Youthful Network

In many cases you can find networks or groups of people with similar interests or characteristics that are loosely organized. They may have even begun to develop a formal process or infrastructure to better work together. If these people are in your core target market or nano-markets, you can leverage this network to benefit your business.

What you will be investing is your expertise, reputation, and personal network to help the community. The group could be a small Meetup group, a specialized Ning network, or a community-focused Facebook page.

With a developing community that has a lot of potential, lack of growth is usually due to lack of committed leadership or lack of expertise and time. Join the community or network and observe at first. You are looking for those members who are most engaged. You also need to identify and connect with the founders of the network.

When a community is new, much of its momentum and growth is due to the founder's enthusiasm and drive. Take time to contribute, participate, and help. Over time you will identify how you can get involved formally as part of the community. At this point, approach the founders or community leaders and, as a trusted member of the community, give them feedback on what you can do to help improve and grow the community.

Some things to consider when being part of someone else's network are:

- ➤ Not everyone wants to hear about gaps or weaknesses in their community, so get permission to give feedback.
- ➤ Know your values and understand their values and vision; they have to be aligned and complimentary.
- ➤ There will be members who are already engaged and possibly doing a poor job; be sensitive to their feelings and pride and also be prepared for politics.
- ➤ Stick to your strengths and expertise; you want to volunteer and contribute in a way that builds your reputation and brand.

Establish a High Profile in an Existing Network

Many of the lessons and strategies that you would use to tap into a youthful network also apply to established communities. There will already be a leadership structure in place in most cases. There will also be nano-markets or groups within the larger network. Seek out the groups of people with whom you can easily establish rapport. These same groups also need to provide an environment in which you can contribute in a way that raises your profile and influence. Your goal is to gain the attention and mind share of the community leaders.

It may take weeks, months, or even a year before the network completely opens up to you. It's well worth the investment to put the time in. Once truly part of the leadership team, you have a valuable network that can help you grow your name and connections. In addition, you will be able to leverage that network when working with other guerrillas.

Network Hubs as Valued Resources

The more great content you create, aggregate, and curate, the more people promote you and link to you. Thus, another way to attract and connect with other guerrillas is through great content that is engaging. As your blog or social destinations grow their number of qualified, engaged visitors, you will begin to have a real asset in many aspects. First, it increases your credibility in the eyes of other guerrillas; they know what it takes to build real loyalty and engaged visitors. In addition to this, if another guerrilla has the same target market, your content and resources can help enhance the value they are already delivering to their clients and prospects.

Tips to create, aggregate, and curate great content:

- ➤ Look for upcoming trends or niche topics that you can specialize in when blogging, creating videos, and so on.
- ➤ Search out other great content creators and create a digest of weekly links on hot topics, trends, or insights.
- ➤ Add content frequently.
- ➤ Add different content such as using multiple media and multiple formats to create contrast and keep your audience engaged.
- ➤ Profile other prominent bloggers and industry leaders.

➤ Make it easy for others to add and share their own thoughts and media on your site.

➤ Look for constant feedback on what type of information and formats people like, and constantly fine tune your content development calendar and strategy.

➤ Evaluate other successful bloggers and content creators (who make a profit, not just drive traffic) and glean lessons from the style and format they use.

Network Hubs as Valued Connectors

Your e-mail list, client base, and connections online are a huge asset. If you have built trust, credibility, and consent with a large portion of your community, your recommendations and referrals will be considered gold.

If you see a need or challenge in one part of your network that could be solved by someone else you're connected to on LinkedIn, Twitter, or Facebook, then introduce the two parties. By solving a problem for one person and giving another an opportunity to develop a new customer relationship, you build massive social capital quickly. The more successful matches you make, the bigger the buzz in the community. People begin to refer to you as the go-to person. It benefits you by generating unsolicited referrals. It also helps when other guerrillas go to the community to do a reference check on you and your track record.

When you find a great service provider, thought leader, or solution, then aggressively and proactively share it with your community. This promotion of valuable people and resources endears you in the eyes of the community and the guerrillas that lead communities.

GUERRILLA ATTRACTION

You don't attract what you want; you attract what you are. If you want to attract better partners and more lucrative clients, you need to do more than just have good targeting criteria. You need to improve and expand who you are as a network hub, trusted resource, and community contributor. This personal growth results in a huge increase in your ability to attract and recruit powerful guerrilla social media marketers as fusion partners.

As a final action step for this chapter, use Figure 9.4 to write down what you could do to enhance your ability to form profitable fusion partnerships.

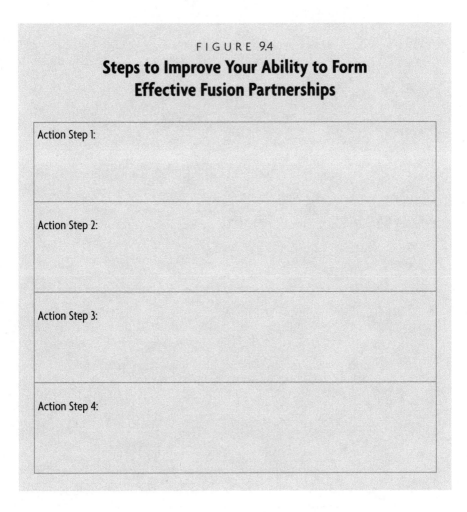

FIGURE 9.4

Steps to Improve Your Ability to Form Effective Fusion Partnerships

Action Step 1:

Action Step 2:

Action Step 3:

Action Step 4:

FIGURE 9.4

Steps to Improve Your Ability to Form
Effective Fusion Partnerships, continued

Action Step 5:
Action Step 6:
Action Step 7:
Action Step 8:
Action Step 9:
Action Step 10:

CHAPTER 10

YOUR GUERRILLA SOCIAL MEDIA ATTACK PLAN

Guerilla marketers are intentional and maximize their resources and return on investment. To do this you need to have a well-thought-out plan and step-by-step calendar of your strategic and tactical movements.

Talent alone is overrated. Charisma and the ability to temporarily wow the crowd online is nothing compared to the strength of a well-implemented plan and strategy. The single biggest waste of money in marketing is not mistakes made due to wrong strategy or choosing poor fusion partners. Nor are the wrong logo, slogan, or packaging the biggest sources of loss. The single biggest and most avoidable marketing cost and loss is quitting.

It takes time, discipline, focus, and guts to follow through on a brilliant guerrilla social media marketing plan. Guerrillas research, listen, and focus in on the right target market and nano-markets. You execute your plan with confidence because you have listened to your clients and prospects with more purpose, meaning, and empathy than anyone else in the marketplace. With this understanding you need to move forward boldly and strategically, not on a whim but with a deep understanding of what it takes to become a community leader, trusted resource, and preferred supplier.

If your marketing plan is too complicated to explain, it is too difficult to execute. A simple plan is easy to execute, easy to share, and easy to sustain. When writing your marketing plan, avoid jargon and padding. Get to the point. Then work the plan with courage, imagination, and a laser focus. To start off you need to write a seven-sentence marketing plan. Later on you expand this plan into a series of calendars and apply the appropriate tools to measure and refine your attack.

THE SEVEN-SENTENCE GUERRILLA SOCIAL MEDIA PLAN

Great ideas, great marketing plans, and brilliant business ideas are everywhere. A great idea alone does not make people successful. A great idea, marketing plan, or business idea that is executed well is what creates success. In order to be a successful guerrilla social media marketer, you must have a simple, easy-to-follow, and easy-to-execute plan. Then you must follow that plan consistently. The seven-sentence guerrilla social media plan is your roadmap to success.

Goals

The first sentence of your guerrilla social media plan tells the purpose of your marketing. Describe very specifically what your guerrilla social media marketing plan is going to achieve. Your goal must be SMART. When setting goals, you need to be able to answer the following questions:

→ Is the goal SMART?
→ Does the goal inspire you?
→ Have you connected or aligned it with your values?

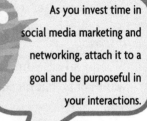

As you invest time in social media marketing and networking, attach it to a goal and be purposeful in your interactions.

SMART Goals

The SMART acronym for goal setting has been used for decades and is still one of the best formulas you can use. SMART stands for:

> *Specific.* The goal is focused.
> *Measurable.* There are benchmarks and metrics in place to measure progress and confirm success.
> *Achievable.* Based on the guerrilla's assets, skills, attitudes, and behaviors, the goal is achievable.
> *Realistic.* Considering all of the factors influencing the goal, it is plausible that it can be achieved.
> *Timely.* Set a specific time for completion. (There are no unrealistic goals, only unrealistic timelines.)

Some examples of SMART goals for a guerrilla social media marketer:

→ Generate 22 quality leads per week that fit my ideal client profile from the social media activities I am doing by August 31.
→ Increase my blog traffic by 1,500 visitors from New York state per day by May 15.

- Increase website revenues by 32 percent within 120 days of starting out my social media launch plan.
- Add 52 new affiliates who meet my ideal partner profile to my affiliate program in the next six months.
- Consistently generate 10 additional reservations per week, at our restaurant using social media and social networking by June 1st.

Inspiring

When you set your goals try not to make them too safe. You don't want goals that far outpace your abilities, but you do want goals that make you stretch. Your goals should keep you up at night (or, more importantly, out of bed early and excited).

> Have a goal so big that it scares your neighbors.

The word inspiring actually comes from the Latin word *inspiro,* which means to breath upon; to breath into; to put the spirit within. As guerrillas if we are to inspire others and put the spirit within them, we must first be inspired ourselves. Be passionate and excited when setting your marketing goals.

Values Alignment

When developing goals it is important to put them through the "values test" to make sure that the goals you are setting will be on purpose. One approach to doing this is to simply list all of the core activities, people, and daily disciplines associated with the goal and then compare them with your values. If 70 percent or more of the activities and disciplines fulfill your core values, then chances are the goal will be an energizing, pleasurable milestone to work toward. If it is less than 70 percent, you should build a new path to the goal or find a new goal that satisfies your core values and drivers.

Competitive Advantage

The second sentence states the competitive advantages you have and the problems you can solve for your target audience. This sentence dictates how you reach your first goal. You need to first know the needs, pains, and goals of your clients and prospects. Then you state how you will uniquely solve their problems or help them reach their goals. It's not enough to save people time or money. Your advantages are your compelling marketing offer.

Don't just promote the same stale benefits everyone else does. Your competitive advantage is the unique way that you deliver your product and service. It's a process of doing business that no one else can deliver as well as you.

This talk about your competitive advantages is most powerful when stated as a solution to a challenge or a problem. It also drives the content of your social media marketing calendar. All of your Tweets, blog posts, videos, photos, and conversations should together tell a story about your competitive advantages.

Target Market

The third sentence identifies your target audience. Establishing and maintaining focus is vital to your success. While most people are comfortable with the 80/20 rule, guerrillas don't want 80 percent of their efforts going to waste. You need a strong understanding of who your ideal clients are. The more specific you can be, the more laser focused and knowledgeable you can become.

Creativity comes from knowledge, and knowledge comes from studying. In this case it's about specializing and focusing on a specific target market until you know it inside and out.

In Chapter 6, Guerrilla Focus, you came up with five to seven main criteria that will help you focus on the right clients and right prospects. Now it's time to define your target market in a single sentence. This will help you quickly determine who you respond to, write for, and monitor online.

Marketing Weapons

The fourth sentence lists the guerrilla social media marketing weapons you plan on using. When you first launch your guerrilla social media marketing attack, your weapons should only take one sentence to list. Picking too many makes it difficult for you to learn and adapt. You must be better than your competitors at using the weapons you choose. This only happens if you first focus, then augment. Eventually you can use your many weapons for different purposes and nano-markets. Initially, pick a maximum of five social media marketing weapons.

Your weapons:

- ➤ Should be used and listened to by your target market
- ➤ Are tools you know how to use effectively or can learn how to use quickly
- ➤ Have a specific social network culture and etiquette that you understand
- ➤ Have been chosen after you have closely monitored and listened to your target market

Positioning

The fifth sentence tells your positioning in the marketplace and the nano-markets that you are focused on. Within your target market there are nano-markets, which you focus on to develop a high level of intimacy and engagement. Individually these small niche groups may not be able to support your business, but collectively they can be very profitable.

Start off with your 140-character positioning statement that you developed in Chapter 2. This positioning statement should dictate your nano-markets. The concept is simple. Instead of being one of many people in a large market, be a dominant player in multiple segments within your broader target market. The next step is to describe in detail your nano-markets for nano-casting. This helps guide the development of your marketing calendar and the specific needs of the audiences you are listening to, talking with, and writing for.

Once chosen, you must stay committed to your specific nano-markets. Consistency and focus in those markets will make you a dominant and profitable player.

Identity

The sixth sentence tells your identity, a vital sentence in a now transparent online world. Your identity must be more than a façade or polished image. It can't be what you would like people to believe about you and your brand. It must honestly and authentically state the personality and identity of your business and include the values you live by. This personality or identity both resonates with and repels certain markets and that's what you want. Your authentic identity is what establishes trust and credibility with your specific audience.

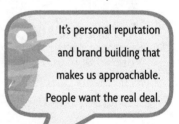

It's personal reputation and brand building that makes us approachable. People want the real deal.

Your identity is more important than ever. From attracting new clients to retaining employees, people want to be part of something that has a purpose beyond just making money. Share and live your values and identity online. Post this sentence where you can see it all the time. Stay committed to authentically living your identity.

Many people don't want to share their true identity online. Their personality or behavior may be socially unacceptable or offensive to their target market. The reality is that with everyone armed with a smartphone or video capture device, your faults and antics are most likely already published online. Instead of hiding, you must do one of three things: Fold up your business and quit, find a client base that approves of your behavior, or improve on your behavior and habits. There's no hiding.

Marketing Budget

The seventh sentence states your marketing budget as a percentage of online profits and includes a projected time investment, because time is life. What is your time worth? Most of your social media investment is time. Is it worth $50 per hour? $200? What would you pay to extend your last days on earth? Don't squander time, or money. Realistically look at the profits you expect to generate, and invest a percentage of that expected profit in time and money. This is where goals, dreams, and aspirations meet hard reality. Get real, focus on the tools that work and the markets that respond, and make sure your investment pays. Then invest a percentage of that expected profit in your marketing plan.

YOUR GUERRILLA MARKETING CALENDAR

Work your plan. Stay focused, and build toward the end goal. Your social media calendar breaks down the brand story you are telling into individual notes of a symphony. On their own, each note or instrument may not be significant, but collectively they ignite the human spirit. Your calendar is your guide to keep you on message, on purpose, and accountable to your own lofty goals. Your guerrilla marketing plan is designed to keep you on track over the long term; your calendar is your short-term accountability tool.

> Blogging tip: Pick a theme or topic for the month. Plan seven to ten blog entries that build up to one core message, event, or action.

Figure 10.1 shows a complete outline of what an individual entrepreneur or staff member should develop to plan and execute his or her guerrilla social media attack. It is broken down weekly and by the social media weapon. First note your overall monthly theme or positioning you want to establish, then indicate how each weapon will be used to support this. In addition to content publishing, your calendar must include guerrilla intelligence or social media monitoring activities.

FIGURE 10.1
Guerrilla Social Media Marketing Calendar

Team Member: _____ Month: _____ Market(s): _____

Overall Theme & Goals for the Month:

Tool/ Media	Week 1	✓	Week 2	✓	Week 3	✓	Week 4	✓
Blog								
Twitter								
Facebook								
LinkedIn								
Video								
Audio Podcast								
Flickr								
Listening tools and terms								
Event (Meetup, LinkedIn, Facebook etc.)								

FIGURE 10.1
Guerrilla Social Media Marketing Calendar, continued

Tool/ Media	Week 1 Eval/Notes	✓	Week 2 Eval/Notes	✓	Week 3 Eval/Notes	✓	Week 4 Eval/Notes	✓
Blog								
Twitter								
Facebook								
LinkedIn								
Video								
Audio Podcast								
Flickr								
Listening tools and terms								
Event (Meetup, LinkedIn, Facebook etc.)								

MAINTAINING YOUR ATTACK

In the world of social media marketing, there are many unexpected opportunities and challenges. Your best-laid plans will not prepare you for what is ahead. The guerrilla social media marketer is committed to his or her long-term goal and understands the power of follow-through. Your success lies in a commitment to the 19 guerrilla social media marketing secrets. This is not an optional commitment. These secrets have been adapted from the 19 guerrilla marketing secrets that have been shared with and applied by literally millions of people. After more than 25 years of guerrillas applying these secrets, one core lesson has been discovered. Guerrillas who want to succeed in the long-term must apply and live all of the secrets.

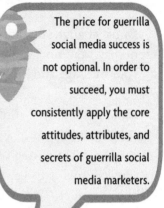

The price for guerrilla social media success is not optional. In order to succeed, you must consistently apply the core attitudes, attributes, and secrets of guerrilla social media marketers.

The 19 guerrilla social media marketing secrets are your official code and core belief system that makes the guerrilla social media marketer successful. Memorize these and make them part of your personal and corporate DNA.

1. Commitment

Mediocre wins over brilliant. The key lesson here is stay the course. Your social media effort, whether blogging, video podcasts, Twitter, or a combination of these tools, must be executed with a one- or two- to ten-year commitment. Stick with it, it will pay big.

2. Investment

Guerrilla marketing is a recession-proof investment if you do it right. It will pay better than any traditional financial investment if you do it right. You need to invest time in social media. Almost all of your investing is not in dollars but in time, energy, imagination, and information.

3. Consistent

Don't change your identity. Brands, relationships, trust, and technology take time for adoption and acceptance. Be consistent with your message and online social media identity.

4. Confident

Instill confidence in your product or service in the customer. Use social media to listen to your customers. Service is anything the customer wants it to be. Listen! Quality is what customers get out of your product. This is great information that can help you provide specific, on-topic, brilliant solutions to your target market's pains.

5. Patient

It takes time for marketing to work. You must be patient. It takes time to master the guerrilla marketing weapons of social media. Be patient as you build a community online. Build roots and a foundation that will be unshakable. Be patient with your target market. Potential customers rush in to use and engage in social media, but they do it in their time frame.

6. Assortment of Weapons

Use diverse tools. Start with a blog or highly socially enabled site. Then use and master or experiment with all the major tools. You can identify over time which ones you have a talent for using and which ones your market responds to best. Today these tools may include:

- Blogging
- Video podcasting (YouTube, Viddler, etc.)
- Facebook

- Linkedin
- Flickr
- Twitter
- Forums
- Ning
- Digg
- StumbleUpon
- FriendFeed
- Google Profiles
- Tumblr
- Ubertor (for real estate)
- Meetup

7. Convenient

Time is money is a lie. Time is life. Don't waste people's time. This is critical. Don't make people work hard to find your information or consume the great content you create. Also, don't waste their time with ten-minute videos when you could say it in three minutes or, even better, three Twitter tweets. Brevity is key in guerrilla social media marketing.

8. Subsequent

The profits come into your business after the initial sale . . . through the follow-up that you do. Always know what's next. Don't write an e-book: write a series of e-books. Don't just solve one customer pain; be in search of the next big thing that can help those who are connected with you.

9. Amazement

Get people's attention by being amazing. Tell stories because stories are not boring. People love stories. That's why they follow you on Twitter; they are following the story of your personal brand 140 characters at a time. Good stories spark passion and hold attention, so get good at using social media and tell stories.

10. Measurement

Measure your success. Use tools like Google Analytics to track the traffic and behavior of those who arrive at your site as a result of your social media activities. Don't just measure only money profits either. Look at happiness, education, network growth, and positive community impact. These are all other forms of profit.

11. Involvement

Listen and engage, or even better, give them platforms to communicate and share. Then jump into the conversation, and let them know that you hear them. This could be building a Ning social network for people who are in your industry. It may be starting a new LinkedIn or Facebook group. You can also use a tool like Meetup to get your online community to meet offline and cement relationships.

12. Dependent

The guerrilla's job is not to compete but to cooperate with other businesses. Market for them in return for their marketing for you. Set up tie-ins with others. Become dependent on others, such as affiliates, to market more so you can invest less. Begin to blog, do interviews, and profile your cooperative competitors online, and many will reciprocate and help you grow your following and client base.

> Build your own affiliate or loyalty program to reward your super fans and advocates.

13. Armament

Arm yourself with all of the social media tools that your customer uses. Also, find new markets through arming yourself with new social networks and mediums.

14. Consent

Permission is number one if you are going to be a guerrilla social media marketer. Take time to build trust and relationships, and never overstate or overstep your relationships online with pitches and unsolicited messaging.

15. Content

Substance wins over style. Give real value and unique content, and do it often with multiple social media weapons. If you want to dominate your marketplace using social media, give more, and give more often. Your community and Google's robots will reward you!

16. Augment

Augment your attack by auditing yourself and your strategy constantly. The world of social media is growing by the millions of members every month. You have to stay up on the tools and demographics of each medium. NHL Superstar Wayne Gretzky attributes his success on the ice to always knowing where the hockey puck was going to be vs. where it was in the moment. He was always ahead of the game. You need to be the same in the social media space. Ask, "What's next?"

17. Congruent

Make sure that all of your tools and messages work together. You should be layering each blog entry, Twitter update, or Facebook post like bricks in a building. They all are valuable and contribute to a greater masterpiece—your brand and reputation.

18. Experiment

You will have little failures before you have one big success. Constantly test and be curious about the psychology behind what motivates and engages your customers,

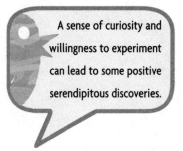

A sense of curiosity and willingness to experiment can lead to some positive serendipitous discoveries.

prospects, and the online communities in which you participate. Remember that penicillin and gunpowder were both invented by accident. Have fun, be engaging and bold, and most importantly observe everything.

19. Implement

The world belongs to those who are willing to implement. Put a solid marketing calendar together that includes core social media disciplines. Blog at least three times per week, update your Twitter status five or more times per day, and spend at least 30 minutes a day proactively listening to your audience.

This last guerrilla social media marketing secret "implement" is the absolute key to your success. This final secret is your silver bullet, the magical ingredient most would-be entrepreneurs and marketers neglect to fully commit to. We have spent an entire book sharing with you the attitudes, attributes, weapons, and strategies of the guerrilla social media marketer. Our work is done, and yours has begun. Your guerrilla social media marketing attack will have a beginning and middle but no end. It is not just a strategy; it's a way of being. Now it's your turn. Write your seven-sentence guerrilla social media marketing plan, fill out this month's calendar, get started—and never look back.

May your future as a guerrilla be one of abundance and happiness!

—Jay Conrad Levinson and Shane Gibson
GuerrillaSocialMediaHQ.com

107
SOCIAL MEDIA
TWEETS

Shane Gibson tweets social media tips every day that he shares with his thousands of Twitter followers. You have seen a selection of these Tweets on the sidebars in this book. These are bite-sized insights that we have archived and are now sharing with you. Take your time and really digest each tip; they're 140 charcters or fewer in length but the principles are vital to your success as a guerrilla social media marketer.

1. Momentum can cause friction. Don't be moving so fast that you forget your community.
2. To build a big network, build many interconnected communities.
3. If you're going to be disruptive, aggressive, and edgy, you also have to be able to take what you dish out—with a smile!
4. A social media listening strategy has to be applied on-going and consistently if you want to maximize ROI.
5. Contrast keeps people interested. With your blog and Twitter content vary tempo, topic, and format.
6. Consistency is a key factor in building your brand; stay present, stay on message, keep listening.
7. Have an integrated marketing plan that includes social media. All media work better augmented.
8. Social media tools are mostly free, but time isn't. Allocate necessary time to make the tools work.
9. Stay curious and you will stay current.
10. Momentum is hard to build and easy to lose. When things start to rock . . . ride the wave and keep pushing.
11. Have a goal or theme, and build a monthly calendar around your social media activities.
12. Crowdsourcing still requires leadership to take ideas and turn them into action. Don't just create fans, equip leaders.
13. Understand tools like FriendFeed, Tumblr, and Ping.fm. They can help you syndicate your messaging for maximum reach.
14. Search engine optimization helps people find you. Integrate an SEO plan with your social media plan.
15. Have a set of guidelines and a social media training program for your staff to ensure that you maximize results.
16. Improve the way you use five tools 10 percent each. Cumulatively it will have a big effect.

17. Easy access to tools like blogging raises the bar for those who want to lead lots of competition.

18. Take massive action when you see a trend that may have large growth potential. You won't win them all . . . but one will do.

19. The best medium is the one your customer likes. Use multiple media.

20. Be open to feedback. Be open to being wrong. Defensiveness isn't all that social.

21. Hone in on and focus on engaging people. Help multiply each other's vision.

22. Many people will quit, shun, and criticize social media marketing when they realize it's actually about leadership.

23. If you keep changing your message, you will keep starting over. Experimenting with your strategic brand is not good.

24. Social media works better when it's incorporated holistically with your entire set of marketing tools.

25. Before listening to someone's social media tips or advice, use social search to verify their credibility.

26. Leadership is influence (John Maxwell) and influence is measured based upon the change and action we create.

27. Use Twitter lists to let people know you're listening.

28. Most social media efforts are abandoned long before their results can be measured.

29. Social media can be used for retaining, developing, and prospecting clients, all aspects of the sales cycle.

30. Get out of your industry vacuum when building strategy. Look for SMM concepts that can be adapted.

31. Want to make good connections? Make value added, thoughtful comments on their blog.

32. Teach your clients about social media, help them get online. It creates more dialogue opportunities.

33. Make it real at least twice a week. Meet offline in person with contacts.

34. Research and test the latest platforms, but don't go down the rabbit hole.

35. Your great idea or blog post is being written in ten different languages by other people right now.

36. Any system or company bent on being exclusive vs. inclusive will fail.

37. Being a thought leader is just as much about selfless contribution as it is about unique dialogue.

38. You don't have to like or use every tool to be successful.

39. Social Media Trend: Brands now need to think global social etiquette when planning their social media strategy.

40. Unique, brief sound bytes produced consistently can yield great results.

41. Once in a while ask your FB and Twitter friends for help. See who steps up. This will tell you a lot.

42. Defining your target market and goals is easy. Engaging them is the challenge.

43. Thank people who comment on your blog via e-mail or Twitter. Let them know you're listening.

44. Search engine optimization can help you rapidly grow your network and connections. Get good at it.

45. Develop a list of your top connections and influencers then make sure you're connected on multiple networks.

46. Have a series of steps planned and measured to track and develop relationships.

47. One of your final steps in the social media sales process is to connect offline, on the phone, or at least one on one virtually.

48. Social media is too new for gurus. We're all amateurs! That's what makes it fun and open.

49. Social media is here to stay and has more relevance and power everyday.
50. Embracing and understanding how to use social media is a core life skill, leadership skill, and career-building skill.
51. Social media is social. It's about helping people connect to people using technology. It embodies truly what the internet was intended for.
52. Social media is not just about technology; it's a new way of leading, thinking, and connecting with other people.
53. Social media belongs to all of us. An ordinary consumer, a front-line employee, a political activist in Iran all have access and a voice.
54. You need different messaging for client retention than you do for attraction.
55. Statistics tend to be a history lesson. Growth and human behavior are rarely linear. Listen to customers and staff.
56. Develop a social media policy and set of guidelines to keep your team on track and on message.
57. You can't force someone to be social; you can only give them the tools and training.
58. Worry less about selling and more about connecting and rapport.
59. Spend time each day promoting and contributing to another blogger's success.
60. What works for you now will only keep working until it is no longer unique. Keep innovating.
61. Polish your work too long and someone will move first with a less perfect work, but they'll get the credit. Publish first.
62. One day we will look back at "social media" as a buzz word. But the best practices will still be in use.
63. Talk and listen to small nodes or groups of people in your larger niche network. Niche broadcasting is not enough.

64. Contribution, help, and kindness are your social currencies that can get you access to great people and great networks.
65. Want to implement your social media plan fast? Think collaboration, not committee.
66. All the details, plans, and tools don't mean much unless you understand people.
67. Stop focusing on being a social media rock star; focus on building a community and a list.
68. Types of social media ROI include: improved staff engagement, quicker response to business challenges, increased frequency contact with clients.
69. There is a lot of hype. Look for truth, verify information, and execute with dependable tools and strategies.
70. Use giveaways that have real value with a variety of paid options to upgrade to. Think customization and options.
71. Some people like lengthy white papers; others learn best through video, audio, or text updates. Use variety.
72. Measure engagement levels, revenues, value-added interactions. Big numbers in views and traffic can lie.
73. Bad customer feedback is a branding opportunity if you handle it right.
74. If you can't be relevant, at least be entertaining!
75. Visit sites outside of your industry and interest areas for new ideas.
76. Constantly look for ways to contribute, and you will never run out of marketing leverage.
77. Social media should be integrated or synced with other marketing activities.
78. Social media is not rocket science. Forget the big words and focus on listening and connecting intimately.
79. Your goal is to become referable, to become credible, and to build a following through value-added interactions.

80. It is not about getting referrals; it is about becoming referable.

81. There are many ways to get followers. A good question to ask is: "How do I create quality connections on Twitter?"

82. Resist the temptation to fill your Facebook friends' inboxes with daily marketing. They will tune you out.

83. Break long blog posts into a series of short posts; it will increase your page views and be more engaging.

84. Prescheduled tweets and blog posts can help you reach audiences in different time zones.

85. It feels great to know people are listening to us and that they care. Let your customers know you're listening.

86. If done right, social media will become a part of your business process not a separate addition.

87. Spend at least as much time listening as you do broadcasting.

88. It's called "social media" for a reason. Be prepared to interact consistently.

89. You can't win the game focusing on the scoreboard. Focus on the game of engagement, and the traffic will come.

90. Study people who are credible with the type of clients you want to attract. Model their strategy.

91. Marketers aren't always synonymous with community builders. Traffic and followers aren't always equal to credibility.

92. If you're an old-school e-mail marketer or pitch artist, there are some habits you need to unlearn.

93. Before you start your campaign, define your market and its pains.

94. Everyone and every company gets off message once in a while. Refocus and learn from it.

95. Leaders of large tribes need to have thick skin and a tolerance for noise.

96. Continually tweak and update your LinkedIn profile; your network will be notified.

97. Social media is changing so quickly that if you stop too long to smell the roses you'll be out of touch.

98. You can't make a robot network for you at a party. Why do you think it can do it for you on the web?

99. You can't please everyone. But know who you are trying to connect with. Get in sync with your audience.

100. Focus on a specific theme in your social media for extended periods of time.

101. Your blog is your home base. All social media should feed your home base.

102. Social media is 90 percent contribution and connection, 10 percent marketing and sales.

103. Social media belongs to the people. They get to make the rules, not the marketer.

104. Take time each month to update your major social media profiles; use keywords that your prospects would search for.

105. Each social network has its own etiquette. Facebook-type behavior doesn't work on LinkedIn.

106. Answer people's comments on your blog or @ replies in Twitter. Social media leadership is about bidirectional communication.

107. Think twice, click once.

GUERRILLA SOCIAL MEDIA MARKETING GLOSSARY

App: Application. Any small program that runs on an existing platform or bigger program, like a survey within Facebook or a fitness planner on your smartphone

CRM: Customer relationship management software. This can be any kind of software that enables you to systematize the way you interact with your customers. Generally the CRM gathers information on the customer via a sign-up form of some kind and stores the information in a database; then, depending on the system's sophistication and how you ask the information to be presented, it can serve up, for instance, all the clients who work within four miles of your office and have incomes over $40,000. This is a highly competitive field for software developers, and you'll find many choices at all price ranges. It's important to pick one you find easy to deal with, rather than one that has the most functions. You can always trade up later, once you've used this tool to grow your success.

Crowdsourcing: This is the practice of letting the public provide you with solutions. Most people, if given the chance and a modicum of respect, are happy to help out with decision making, directions, referrals, and advice. Give them the opportunity as often as you can. Not only can you often get excellent, objective advice but it also makes people feel much more engaged with you and your projects.

Domain/subdomain: These terms refer to the address on the internet of any given site. An example of a domain is Whatever.com; an example of a subdomain is Something.Whatever.com. For brand recognition reasons, it's almost always better for your site to have a unique domain or a subdomain of your main website, like Mysite.com or Mysite.com/blog rather than Whatever.Blogspot.com or Whatever.Wordpress.com. It not only looks more professional, it's easier to remember and for technical reasons far more transportable. Should you change site hosts in the future, you can use the unique domain or subdomain in your new webspace and your readers don't need to know anything has changed. If you've previously used Whatever.Blogspot.com and you move to Whatever.com in a new webspace, you'll need to redirect your readers and risk losing them.

Google: Way more than a search engine! Google is a bundle of free online services including Blogspot.com blog host, document and file hosting, Groups, Gmail e-mail service, Google Wave, Google Buzz, and a never-ending stream of new apps and services. It's worthwhile to read the Google blog or one of the blogs that exists to explain these services to nontechies. They can be very powerful tools, but only if you know how to use them.

Guerrilla marketing: It is about achieving conventional business goals using nonconventional means. It is a movement and approach that allows creative, entrepreneurial individuals to compete with big companies and market leaders by using creativity, innovation, community, and relationships instead of big budgets to achieve marketing objectives.

Hardware: Machinery of any kind. Social media hardware includes anything from an iPhone to a desktop computer.

Hosting: This is to websites what being a landlord is to renters. The web host is a company that owns a server on which websites can be hosted. They generally charge a monthly fee for the service. Websites cannot be hosted on regular computers, by the way, because they are not designed for that function. Shop around for a web host and realize that reliability, not cost, is the key factor in choosing a host. Word of mouth is important for making a good decision.

Mac: Macintosh computers, a highly successful line of computers from Apple, which introduced icon-based computer navigation to the public. Apple products are known for their beautiful design and ease of use.

Nano-: Tiny and precisely defined when compared to broad-based marketing efforts and targets. This prefix can be attached to any number of words and changes their meaning appropriately. An example of "nano-casting" would be posting information about a men's shoe sale at an upscale store in a particular suburb, to draw the attention of high-income professional men in that specific area.

Noob: You'll hear the word "noob" a lot if you're learning social media. It means a newcomer, and has overtones of scorn. Back in the day, the internet was a land where geeks ruled, and no hegemony gives up control to the people without a fight. The word "noob" is just about the last weapon they have to use against you;

just let it roll off your back and get on with learning to use social media effectively. One of the key skills is, in fact, the ability to grow a thick skin.

Open source: An open-source program is one where the actual lines of code are not secret; they are freely shared so that developers and enthusiasts can improve and update the program. This means they can frequently be more cutting edge than proprietary software. The rapid speed of development when volunteers around the world get involved means that open-source programs are developed much faster and come to market more quickly than other programs. Security tends to be excellent because so many people test so many different aspects of security.

PC: It's short for personal computer and is generally taken to refer to all desktop or laptop computers that are not Apple products, regardless of what kind of software they run.

Photoshop: The grandfather of graphic programs, this is a professional-level graphic tool that allows you to do an incredible variety of things with images. Unfortunately, it is not intuitive to use and may be overkill for guerrilla social media marketers. If you're already a graphic designer, you're undoubtedly fluent in Photoshop; otherwise, it's best to stick to something simpler like Gimp or free online services such as Picnik.

Plug-ins: Like apps, these are small programs that are added on to your existing software to increase its functionality. Plug-ins are common for WordPress, Firefox, and open-source programs, and can greatly increase the effectiveness of basic programs.

Podcast: These can be either audio-only or video (also called a vlog). Analogous to either radio or tv, they can be short, like a commercial, or fully show-length, depending on your needs and intentions. Current technology makes these easy and cheap to produce while maintaining a professional look and sound.

PowerPoint: Simply put, PowerPoint is the way presentations communicate information. It's the number-one software for developing presentation slides, and can repackage your slides so you can upload them to the web on slideshow platforms like Slideshare. Slides are becoming more and more important as the reach of any given presentation now includes people who are not physically present and may only have access to your slides. Make sure your slides explain things well because good slides testify to your own thoroughness as a presenter.

Real time: This simply means that material is posted/remarked on as it happens. Livestreamed video, where people can view what's happening right now, is one example. Twitter can offer up real-time commentary as well as more thoughtful, time-independent posts.

Smartphone: A smartphone is a cellphone with computer-like functionality. Google produces the Android operating system that is used on many smartphones, and Apple, of course, produces the iPhone with its proprietary operating system. Other developers produce apps that further increase the functionality of these smartphones. The difference between these and regular cellphones is the ability to add and use apps to customize the phone. It's more than just the sum of its hardware and software out of the box.

Social media: It is any tool or pathway for bidirectional communications that includes one of a wide variety of new technologies, usually internet-based. Most of the tools guerrillas focus on are free or nearly free. Examples include Twitter, Facebook, blogs, YouTube, and even e-mail. The key thing to remember about social media: it is *social*.

Social networking: Not just standing around a hotel ballroom with canapés, social networking takes place online on certain websites designed specifically for it, like Facebook (to connect with friends), LinkedIn (to connect with colleagues and clients), Tumblr (to connect with hipsters), as well as in blog comments on Twitter and any other Web 2.0 site that allows the readers to speak out.

Software: These are programs that run on hardware. Programs are just sets of instructions that tell a piece of hardware what to do when it gets certain inputs, like the pressing of a button. It's software that adds versatility to hardware. A computer can do as many things as its software allows; it cannot do anything it does not have the programming to accomplish.

Theme: Any website, even just a Twitter profile page, has a certain web design. It's to your advantage to make sure all your sites/pages/profiles have a pleasing and (more importantly) clear design. The temptation to try to do this yourself is great, but is generally unnecessary because there are many thousands of free or inexpensive, attractive, and safe themes you can simply download, then apply to your website. Unless you're a talented designer, customizing your design yourself may not be the best plan.

Troll: A troll is someone who comments on your blog, hits you up on Twitter, posts on your Facebook page, or takes any other action in a way that is specifically designed for no other reason than to insult you or cause you trouble. Thanks to the democratization of tech, trolls are now vastly outnumbered by people who behave better. You are certain to encounter trolls at some point, but they are not as terrifying as they used to be, nor are they powerful.

Tweetup: It's a casual get-together where the invitation is sent out on Twitter. The etiquette is: if you read the tweet, you're invited. No RSVP is necessary, and typically there is no host as such. People simply show up at whatever restaurant, stadium, or plaza hosts the tweetup and pay for what they order. Think of it as a socially focused flashmob where you don't have to get dispersed by the police.

Twitter: It's an indispensible social media site where posts are limited to text 140 characters in length, including URLs. You can add media like audio, photos, and video to your tweets (or posts) by using a third-party service like TwitPic. Twitter distinguished itself during the 2010 Olympics as the home of live-event coverage, and it is extremely useful for integrating online life with face-to-face meetings. Because it is conversational, people feel they already know you and are much more likely to say yes to a meeting.

URL: The URL of any website is just the exact web address of the particular page or post. That includes everything in the browser bar space, including the http. Modern software is smart enough that you don't need to type http or www and most know that you can usually find the page you're looking for without it, but when you are asked for your URL, give out the entire thing. Many programs only make a clickable link if they see "http" in the front.

User-generated content: It's much like crowdsourcing; but in this case the people coming to your site are also making and posting content. An example is ICanHasCheezburger.com, where people caption and upload pictures and the site simply features these contributions and allows voting on them.

Web 2.0: This refers to any interactive site or platform online where communication goes out not only from the author but also back to the author from the audience. The powerful engagement that this fosters is the reason why Web 2.0 sites are the dominant sites on the web right now, and increasingly directing the culture.

Web 3.0: This is just a buzzword applied to any site or offering that the marketer wants to make seem particularly exciting. It does not currently actually mean anything; it just sounds newer and flashier than Web 2.0.

Webcam: A particular kind of video camera optimized for the internet, it is particularly easy to use, but because the quality of the video it outputs is no greater than the typical monitor can display, it is not adaptable for high-quality video production.

Web crawler: This is a program used by search engines (among others) to travel all over the web looking for certain things such as pages, links, etc. Its job is to literally crawl over the entire web looking for whatever specific information it's been programmed to find. Web crawlers are often referred to as spiders or bots as well (bots being short for "robots"). Rather than stomping them out, they should be actively encouraged.

White-labeled Nnetworks: These are just individually hosted networks that have been tested by thousands or tens of thousands of people around the world and found to be safe and easy to use. They won't put viruses on your computer; they won't spam your readers; they are trustworthy. Ning and BuddyPress are two examples of white-labeled networks.

Wifi: It is a particular kind of wireless internet connectivity, and currently the dominant one worldwide. When you're at the café and surfing the internet on your laptop, you're using wifi. Phones can surf the net using wifi OR the wireless cellphone connection, which makes them terrific backups. Cellphone coverage is much broader than wifi coverage, even in cities. Wifi systems can be closed, requiring a password, or open and available to all.

XML: Documents posted online have to be encoded digitally somehow, and XML is a set of rules or "grammar" for that coding. It's a little more technical than we typically get in guerrilla social media marketing; what you need to know is that it's one standard way to convey information online at the code level. When you see terms like "XML sitemap," it tells you that this is the way your sitemap is written so Google and other search engines can understand it easily.

YouTube: the world's largest video-sharing site where people upload their videos. You can allow or disallow comments, annotations, and video responses to your videos, and you can even make them private if they're not ready for prime time.

INDEX